THE SCARLET AND THE BLACK

Monsignor Hugh O'Flaherty

J. P. Gallagher

THE SCARLET
AND THE BLACK

The True Story of
Monsignor Hugh O'Flaherty,
Hero of the Vatican Underground

IGNATIUS PRESS   SAN FRANCISCO

Originally published by Coward-McCann, Inc. as:
Scarlet Pimpernel of the Vatican
© 1967 by J. P. Gallagher

Reprinted with permission
of Souvenir Press, Ltd., London

Photograph: "Cobbles of Via della Conciliazione, Vatican City, Rome"
© iStockphoto.com
Photograph: "Priest in Venice, San Marco Square"
© iStockphoto.com

Cover design by John Herreid

Published 2009 by Ignatius Press
ISBN 978-1-58617-409-5
Library of Congress Control Number 2009930111
Printed in the United States of America ⊗

CONTENTS

An aerial view of Vatican City 1962, showing St. Peter's Square, the scene of so many of O'Flaherty's adventures.

PREFACE

One way or another, this story has been nine years in preparation. It began when I first met Monsignor O'Flaherty at the Holy Office in autumn 1958 and christened him "Scarlet Pimpernel of the Vatican" in a newspaper article. Quite apart from gathering the detailed information he always refused to reveal himself, securing it instead from people scattered around the world, the major task has been to sort fact from fiction, for even today—more than twenty years after the war—the very mention of O'Flaherty's name in Rome is enough to start a flood of reminiscence, much of it owing more to affection than accuracy. To the Romans and to the thousands of men he saved he remains one of the great heroes of World War II.

Many people have helped with information, guidance and correction and I have specially to thank His Eminence Cardinal Alfredo Ottaviani, Head of the Congregation for the Doctrine of the Faith; His Grace Dr. Thomas Ryan, Bishop of Clonfert, Ireland; the Rt. Rev. Monsignor M. F. Toal, of the Collegio Teutonicum, Rome; the Rev. Father Francis Joy, S.J., Rector of Clongowes Wood College, Ireland; the Rev. Father R. F. Roche, S.J., Rector of Mungret College, Ireland; the Rev. Brother F. Brendan, F.S.C., Superior of the De La Salle College, Waterford, Ireland; Field Marshal the Earl Alexander of Tunis; Mr. Sean Brady; Lt.-Col. Sam Derry; Major Colin Lesslie; Mrs. Gemma Sands, neé Chevalier; and Mrs. Bridie Sheehan, Monsignor O'Flaherty's sister.

Among books consulted were *Roma Felix*, Monsignor O'Flaherty's own guide to Rome; *The Rome Escape Line* by Lt.-Col. S. I. Derry, D.S.O., M.C. (London: George G. Harrap and Co., 1960); *Be Not Fearful* by Lt.-Col. John Furman, M.C. (London: Anthony Blond, 1959); *Crown of Glory* by Alden Hatch and Seamus Walshe (London: William Heinemann, 1956); *John XXIII* by Father Francis J. X. Murphy, C.Ss.R. (London: Herbert Jenkins, 1959); *The Irish Republic* by Dorothy MacArdle (London: Victor Gollancz, 1937); and *The Second World War* by Winston S. Churchill (London: Cassell and Co., 1951).

J. P. Gallagher

CHAPTER ONE

The Anti-British Youth

JUST AFTER EIGHT o'clock on one cool March morning in
1944, during the German military occupation of Rome, a
large black sedan drove swiftly and smoothly up the Via
della Conciliazione toward St. Peter's Basilica. It did not
enter the immense piazza but stopped instead beside a white
line painted on the ground to link the two arms of the
Bernini Colonnade. Standing by the line were four German paratroopers, cradling submachine guns. Out of the
car stepped Colonel Herbert Kappler, commander of German SS forces in Rome, followed by two men in plain clothes
but bearing the unmistakable stamp of the Gestapo. Colonel Kappler pointed across the Piazza to the far left-hand
corner of the twenty-two steps leading up to the entrances
to the Basilica. Half in the shadows on the top step stood
the tall figure of a Monsignor of the Catholic Church, in
low-crowned, black hat and long, black robe with red fac-
ings. At more than three-hundred-yards distance his face
could not be distinguished, but the sunlight flashed off his
glasses as he lifted his head from the devotional book he
had been reading to watch the new arrivals. Romans were
moving slowly up and down the steps. It was a peaceful
scene, and a fantastic background for a murder plot. For
Colonel Kappler had not arrived to inspect the Nazi guards—
but to plan an assassination.

Now he pointed toward the figure on the steps and said to his men, "That is he—Monsignor Hugh O'Flaherty, a mad Irish priest, but dangerous, too dangerous to live. He has given us more trouble than any other man in Rome and it must stop. He knows he will be arrested if we catch him outside Vatican territory and we have so far failed to lure him across that line, or spot him when he has slipped away into the city, which he does whenever he feels like it! Since we can't take him frontally, we shall try from the rear. Listen carefully. He does not know you . . . you have never been on duty here before? No . . . that is good. Tomorrow you will attend service in St. Peter's. It is a feast day of some sort so there will be plenty of people. As they start to come out you will come out also, but use the door immediately behind where O'Flaherty stands now. Seize him, hustle him down the steps and across the line. When you get him away and into a side street free him . . . for a moment. I don't want to see him alive again and we certainly don't want any formal trials. He will have been 'shot while escaping'. Understood?"

The two Gestapo men nodded silently. They understood very well. This was a routine in which they were fully trained. It was not a very clever plot, but it was all that a frustrated and furious Kappler could think of.

On the evening of the same day a dapper little man in black jacket and gray pin-striped trousers, with black tie and white wing collar, entered O'Flaherty's small office and said, "Monsignor, a little problem has come up. You know our friend Giuseppe, our 'contact' in the Questura? Well he's just told me that Kappler has some amiable plans to kidnap you tomorrow. I don't know exactly how, but I think you'd better stay off the steps for a day or two!"

O'Flaherty rose from his desk to his full height of six feet two inches, a powerful man of over two hundred pounds, forty-six years old, one-time athlete and amateur boxer, and gave his great booming laugh.

"What, me boy, and let them think I'm afraid? So long as they don't use guns I can tackle any two or three of them with ease—though a scrap would be a bit undignified on the very steps of St. Peter's itself, would it not?"

The little man, whose name was John May, coughed delicately. "Monsignor," he said, "you have a point. If the Nazis can't try this on one day they'll have a go another time and perhaps we won't get warning on that occasion. Giuseppe can't be expected to get to know everything always. I think Kappler needs a lesson. If you would leave it to me, Monsignor . . ."

"I don't want to know anything about your plans, John", smiled O'Flaherty. "But I will be there in the morning just as usual."

May left nothing to chance. He got a message through to Giuseppe and early the next morning the young informant went to Mass in St. Peter's—with the non-Catholic May.

Immediately inside the main door of St. Peter's, on the right-hand side, is the first of the forty-four altars in the enormous Basilica, which can hold one hundred thousand people. Here, in the chapel of Michelangelo's *Pieta*, the only work of the master to bear his name, stood the two plainclothes SS men, heads hypocritically bowed, hands clasped together in front of them. Giuseppe gestured toward them and May threw a glance to four Swiss Guards who had appeared just inside the doors. The Basilica was filled with the susurration of a score or more priests whispering their Masses, the faint click of women's shoes on marble as people came from the altar rails after Communion, the ethereal tinkle of sanctuary bells. Softly, too, the Swiss Guards moved forward, one each to stand on the left and right of the SS men and two behind them. A tap on the shoulder of each man and an emphatic motion toward the doors, the Germans shrugged, and went quietly.

It is true that they went out as planned by the door just behind O'Flaherty's post, but they walked meekly, flanked by the powerful Guards and followed by an anticipatorially smiling May. The Monsignor stood aside to let them pass, his intense blue eyes flashing merrily behind the cheap steel-rimmed spectacles he always wore. Down the steps they were led, heading toward the usual line of Nazi paratroopers on the perimeter. But halfway across the piazza May muttered something to the Guard commander and the Germans, looking puzzled now, were steered gently but firmly over to a corner of the colonnade giving access to the street in which the Holy Office stands. As they passed out on the far side of the colonnade they were still on extraterritorial land and the paratroopers, even if they had recognized Kappler's civilians, could do nothing about it. May had arranged his own reception committee—of Yugoslavians, whose hatred for Germans was relentless and undying. It was the SS men who were jostled down a side street and it was a very battered and bruised pair who reported yet another failure to Kappler later that morning.

Once again the scourge of the Germans in Rome, the most "wanted" man in the Eternal City, had won. O'Flaherty, the genial, gentle, guileless priest, was the Pimpernel of the Vatican, robed in scarlet and black, a strangely paradoxical man who for so long detested the British yet saved more Allied lives than any other single person in World War II. Operating an amazing rescue network from inside Rome's German College itself, with his own secret "line" to SS headquarters, he defiantly stalked the city by day and by night, taunting the Germans by his very presence, standing alone on the steps of St. Peter's waiting for those in trouble to come to him and be saved from imprisonment, torture and possibly death. On any given night of the winter of 1943–1944, for example, he would have between one hundred and two hundred escaped prisoners, from privates to generals—hidden in the homes of anti-Fascist Romans, in convents and in monasteries, their lives a succession of hair's-breadth escapes, often in O'Flaherty's own monsignorial robes, sometimes uproariously impudent.

Hugh Joseph O'Flaherty was born at Killarney, County Kerry, on February 28, 1898, the eldest child of Margaret and James O'Flaherty. Two more boys and one girl followed. All the boys went to school at the monastery in Killarney town, run by the Presentation Brothers. Apparently Hugh had wanted to be a priest from an early age, but when he was fifteen he secured a junior teaching post at the monastery and taught there for three years. He won a King's Scholarship and two years' free training at the Waterford College of the Brothers of Saint John Baptist de la Salle, but he caught pleurisy in the summer of 1918 and failed his final examination for the diploma in teaching. Still determined to become a priest, he applied for admission to an institution in Limerick, the Apostolic School of the Sacred Heart, otherwise known as Mungret College, which trained boys for missionary work. Run by the Jesuit Order, it offered bursaries to approved boys between the ages of fourteen and eighteen.

Although he was two years past the upper age limit, O'Flaherty was admitted on August 30, 1918. He was graded as very proficient in English and commercial subjects but had so far done no Latin, and so, although tall and massive already when he arrived at Mungret, he had at first to sit with the boys in the youngest class. But by Christmas 1919 he was first in the senior grade Pass Class. On the whole he was more distinguished as an athlete and sportsman than at his studies. He had learned to play golf at Killarney and Waterford, and this became an abiding passion with him. He was a formidable boxer, good handball player and nearly as good at hurling. He was also a fierce nationalist at a time when Ireland was fighting for her very nationhood.

One incident of O'Flaherty's days at Mungret remains well-remembered by his contemporaries. Low, yellow-gray storm clouds rolling in from the Atlantic darkened the school refectory that December morning in 1920. But nothing could dampen the bubbling spirits of the forty-five or so teenage boys who were finishing breakfast on the day they were breaking up for the Christmas holidays. Normally a proper sense of decorum is expected from Mungret students at meals, as at other times, but on this occasion the prefects indulgently ignored the gaiety, the high buzz of excited conversation, the occasional giggles that burst through, even the open laughter that came from one table where a dozen boys were listening to a joke being told by the tall, gangling, raw-boned O'Flaherty. He finished his story with his enormous laugh and was clearly about to embark on another anecdote when the prefect who was distributing the morning mail handed a letter over his shoulder. O'Flaherty began to read it. The smile vanished, his ruddy face grew dark with anger and, sensing his mood, the others at the table stopped talking to watch him.

"Chris Lucy has been shot by the Tans", he said at last, and the cheerful young faces around him sobered instantly. "That's the fourth Mungret lad they've killed this year."

The year 1920 was the worst in Irish history for centuries. The British were fighting the Irish uprising not only with Regular Army forces and Auxiliaries but also with the "Black and Tans", thus labelled from their mixed uniforms. This ignoble force included freed jailbirds and thugs of every description, indisciplined slaughterers whose conduct led to the resignation of many British Army officers ashamed of the atrocities the "Tans" committed. The boys at the table where O'Flaherty sat were all ardent Republicans—it was known as the "IRA Table"—and now they yelled, as they had done before in the past months, "One day we'll sink the whole British Navy!" And a dozen fists emphatically thumped on the table, setting the crockery rattling in a boyish but heartfelt outburst. Knowing what this meant, the faces of some other lads in the refectory hardened, some smiled tolerantly, others sniggered unthinkingly, the few English boys scowled or looked embarrassed. O'Flaherty turned to his neighbor and muttered with quiet fury, "And the English called the Germans 'Huns' during the war! It's a pity the Germans didn't win, and hang Lloyd George and the whole British Cabinet from the lampposts of Whitehall!"

Hard, even vicious words for a young would-be priest, but they were bitter days in Ireland. The *Mungret Journal* for 1920 carried not only the obituary notices of the four young men to whom O'Flaherty had referred (one shot before his mother's eyes) but also the day-by-day school diary which O'Flaherty helped to write. This included such notes as: "November 1. Feast of All Saints. Our Free Day today was saddened by the news wired to Father Rector by Kevin Barry's mother that her brave son had died at the dawn of the day. We thought of him as one of ourselves, a schoolboy. Shall not his hero's death be always an inspiration for Irish boys?" Undergraduate Kevin Barry was hanged in Mountjoy Jail, Dublin, though only 18, and probably his death did more than any one other thing to stiffen Irish resistance and bring volunteers flocking to the ranks of the Irish Republican Army. On the same day that Barry died ignominiously, Ellen Quin was shot dead by men of the Royal Irish Constabulary. She had been sitting on her garden wall with her baby in her arms when the police fired from a passing truck.

The military inquiry reported that the shooting was "a precautionary measure". Day after day through November and December 1920, men, women and children were butchered—eight-year-old Annie O'Neill was killed when shots were fired from a truck into a group standing peacefully in a gateway ... the body of Father Michael Griffin was found in a Galway bog ... the Auxiliaries stopped Canon Magner on a road near Bandon, County Cork, where he was talking with Timothy Crowley and a motorist who had paused for some reason. The Auxiliaries began to abuse the three men and suddenly Cadet Harte shot Crowley dead. When the Canon began an outraged protest, Harte shot him dead also. The motorist happened to be a Resident Magistrate and he was able to force through an inquiry. Harte was found "guilty but insane" and nobody else was charged.

This sort of thing and countless other barbarities naturally had a profound influence on young Irish students. O'Flaherty's own father had been a Sergeant in the Royal Irish Constabulary but was among the hundreds of men who resigned from the Force rather than help massacre their own people. (In two months alone in 1920, 556 R.I.C. men and 313 magistrates resigned their offices under the Crown.) It was, then, no wonder that O'Flaherty, who was twenty-two at this time and no immature boy, developed an implacable hostility to all things English, an attitude he carried with him to some degree until his death.

O'Flaherty had his own direct brush with the British forces on March 7, 1921, the feast of Saint Thomas and a school holiday. With two friends, he had decided to walk the three miles into Limerick to pray at the cathedral and visit the homes of George Clancy, mayor of Limerick, and his predecessor in office, Michael O'Callaghan, who had been deliberately selected as leading citizens and shot dead in their own homes the previous night. Everyone who called at the two houses of mourning that day was watched and followed. As the three students were passing the police barracks in Limerick's William Street, five Black and Tans surrounded them.

"Into the barracks" ordered the leader. Inside, the Tans questioned the young men about their visit to the city and made it quite clear that they did not believe they were theological students, of all things. Getting no response from the students, the Tans, ever on knife-edge, began to lose their tempers and might well have taken their usual drastic action with suspects, when a police inspector rushed into the room. The Rector of Mungret College, warned by a passerby that three of his students had been arrested, had telephoned to demand their instant release. Reluctantly the Tans let their prisoners go.

Something of O'Flaherty's attitude to life and especially his Irish nationalism emerged in an essay he wrote for the *Mungret Journal* in 1921, an essay which won a prize offered by Father John Nicholson of Laramie, Wyoming. Father Nicholson had been in Europe during much of the recent war, recuperating from an illness. In Germany he met Sir Roger Casement and helped him with his attempt to form an "Irish Brigade" among the Irish prisoners-of-war in Limburg Camp, which Casement hoped he could use for an invasion of Ireland backed by German troops. Only fifty-two men joined, however, and the whole project collapsed.

Father Nicholson's annual prize was offered for the best essay on "the economic reconstruction of Ireland".

O'Flaherty's essay was entitled: "The best means of spreading Irish culture". He defined culture as "the intellectual uplifting of each individual in the State with the inculcation of a pure love of country, in such manner that the nation as a whole benefits—morally, mentally, physically, and materially". Demanding an Irish (not English) language culture, he pleaded for "successful" Irish theater, music and dancing. "The modern music in our halls has not much soul or spirit in it", he went on. "Its utter inability to exist shows how useless it is. Today it delights but tomorrow it vanishes. The music is degenerating, but dancing is still more demoralising. In some English halls it is no longer recognised as a means of recreation or of physical development. Therefore we must teach our people to ban those dances, which are the unchristian productions of the African savages."

At Christmas 1921, O'Flaherty learned that he had been "adopted" by the Cape Town Vicariate in South Africa, and would be sent to Rome to start his theological studies. He arrived in Rome shortly after Pope Benedict XV died in January 1922, but he was to be affected immediately by some of the last major decisions to be taken by Benedict.

The Pope had been concerned, perhaps above all other problems, with the simple battle to preserve Catholicism in far-flung areas of the world where postwar ideological revolutions, following the Russian model, were creating vast pockets of atheistic materialism. Historically the task of converting pagans belonged to the Sacred Congregation for the Propagation of the Faith. For *reconversion*, a task reminiscent of the Propaganda Fide's battles in the sixteenth century, Pope Benedict wanted new blood—aggressive fighting men. He therefore planned a thorough reorganization of the

Congregation, and to combat the lethargic and the diehards he brought in Monsignor Angelo Roncalli (who was to become Pope John XXIII). At the same time fresh blood was to be injected into the Congregation's own training school, the Urban College, established by Pope Urban VIII in 1627 to fight the apostasies and heresies of the era. It was to the Propaganda College that young Hugh O'Flaherty was sent, to mingle with men from thirty-six nations training for the mission fields around the world.

For three years O'Flaherty studied hard (while Monsignor Roncalli stumped Europe to shake new life into the men and women who supported the Congregation with prayers and money). For one who had by no means been brilliant at school, O'Flaherty's achievement in getting his Bachelor degree in Theology in but one year was remarkable and it certainly surprised his former teachers at Mungret! He was ordained priest on December 20, 1925, and because he had gone to Rome sponsored by the Cape Town Vicariate, he naturally expected to be sent to the African missions. But the Rector of the Propaganda College, Monsignor Dini, had had his eye on the young man for some time, and O'Flaherty was as startled as were the other 120 or so students to find himself at once appointed Vice Rector, third in command, an extraordinarily high position and immense honor for a priest still only twenty-eight. Not only was he the same age as many of the students, he was the first Irishman in memory to be appointed to anything like such an important office in Rome. For the next two years O'Flaherty worked at the Propaganda College, collecting meanwhile his triple Doctorates of Divinity, Canon Law and Philosophy. Then, in 1934, Monsignor Dini was appointed Apostolic Delegate to Egypt and he took with him as secretary his protégé, now himself a monsignor. However, Dini suddenly died and O'Flaherty had to take over as Charge d'Affaires, which he did with considerable efficiency. He was now part of the Vatician Diplomatic Service and, on his return to Rome early in 1935, he was sent by Cardinal Pacelli (later Pope Pius XII) as secretary to the Apostolic Delegate to the adjacent republics of Haiti and San Domingo in the Caribbean. In the year that he spent there O'Flaherty was decorated by the president of each republic—Haiti for famine relief work after disastrous floods, San Domingo for successfully arbitrating on an ancient frontier dispute between the two tiny countries and settling an agreed boundary. It was said that it was the excellence of his game of golf that enabled him to wangle some very special diplomatic concessions out of an American Admiral—which sounds like O'Flaherty. In 1936 he was brought back to Rome, and then sent to Czechoslovakia, a land already under the shadow of the Swastika. Whatever this mission was, O'Flaherty never told his friends what he was doing there until January 1938; at that time he was summoned to Rome again and given a new appointment—in the Holy Office.

CHAPTER TWO

God's Traveller

IF THE Sacred Congregation for the Propagation of the Faith
had needed new life, new men and fresh direction to cope
with problems after World War I, it was equally important
for the Sacred Congregation of the Holy Office, supreme
arbiter under the Popes of faith and morals, lineal successor
to the Inquisition, and by 1938 meeting greater challenges
than ever in its history. The development of radio; the vast
production of books, newspapers and magazines for an
increasingly literate world; "modern thinking" on sex,
divorce, every subject indeed, all clashed with the teachings
of the Church, which were defended by the Holy Office
(whose title was changed in 1966 to Congregation for the
Doctrine of the Faith). The Roman Inquisition was established on July 21, 1542, as a final court of appeal of six
cardinals for trials concerning the Faith and a court for the
preliminary examination of all other cases that required reference to the Pope himself. In Fr. O'Flaherty's time the
Holy Office, among its other functions, operated the Catholic Church's supreme court of justice, the tribunal that
decides matrimonial and occasional criminal cases, and every
Catholic was subject to it except the Cardinals, who could
be judged only by the Pope. The consultors and other officials of the Holy Office, aided by the notaries, men like
O'Flaherty, examined challenges to the Faith, arguments on

morals and all aspects of the Church's teaching and doctrine. It is they who inquired into the veracity or otherwise of claimed visions and miracles, who dealt with controversial books and who ruled on the majority of applications for the nullification of marriage or other marital problems. Their work was conducted under the strictest secrecy (called the Secret of the Holy Office) with automatic excommunication for any violation, however slight, however accidental or indirect. The officials left their desks in the Palace of the Holy Office just outside the walls of the Vatican, on the left-hand side of the Bernini Colonnade, every Monday for a conference at which they sorted out the problems that had to be referred to the Cardinal Secretary of State and every Cardinal who lived in Rome, who met each Wednesday.

It was here then, with this most secretive, most unbending, most powerful arm of the Church, that O'Flaherty was to spend almost a quarter of a century, becoming Head Notary when Monsignor Jorio was made a Cardinal. The *Primo Notario* is the man who drafts all decisions of the Holy Office into their final form and signs them. The man who was himself an Inquisitor of Rome was also to spend a heroic year cheating and defying the Nazi and Fascist inquisitors, torturers and jailers. Head of the Holy Office in 1938 was Monsignor Alfredo Ottaviani, two years younger than O'Flaherty, and the tenth of the eleven children of a Roman baker. As Cardinal Ottaviani, it was he who announced the election of Pope Paul VI and crowned him. Ottaviani, long regarded as a stickler for convention and rules, rather surprisingly developed an immense regard for the ebullient Irishman and remained his closest friend and supporter at the Holy Office until O'Flaherty died.

Though few people realized it, it was largely arising out of his work at the Holy Office that O'Flaherty now entered on those aspects of his career which were to cause many a prim Vatican eyebrow to be raised at the very mention of the name of the towering Monsignor who rapidly became one of the idols of Roman society. He was a poor bridge player but thought nothing of playing the night through, and, by now, an accomplished golfer. Practically disinterested in food except as a basic necessity of life, he nonetheless adored parties ... and the princesses and duchesses and countesses adored the so-different cleric with the soft brogue, the huge grin and tremendous sense of humor. It was he who taught Mussolini's son-in-law, the ill-fated Count Ciano, to play at Rome Golf Club, known when O'Flaherty first joined it in 1926 as The British Club; and he also played frequently there with ex-King Alfonso of Spain. This in itself gave him a unique entrée to Italy's top people, something that was to prove invaluable to him and to the Allies in a very few years. With his height and weight he was also a very good boxer. All this, and his position for a time as amateur golf champion of Italy, did nothing to endear him to some of the Vatican Establishment, particularly since it was against the rules of the Diocese of Rome for a priest to play golf! Ottaviani did not mind, however, for he knew that his assistant was turning out to be a first-class Vatican diplomat, indeed, a sort of special agent.

Though his official rank, until 1946, was *Scrittore*, or Writer, O'Flaherty was the man employed for many of the endless confidential talks with members of the United States hierarchy when they came to Rome with their difficulties, nearly always problems which fell within the province of the Holy Office to settle. These talks generally took place in hotels or at dinner parties, and the Holy Office found their highly informal "ambassador", with his ever-widening circle of contacts in high places, extremely valuable.

O'Flaherty himself often wondered about his role at the Holy Office. Though he never lacked incisiveness or confidence in decisions he had reached, he was a very humble man, with no opinion at all of his own attainments. He told one of the British officers he was hiding in the Vatican, "I suppose life is pretty dull for you here. Come and talk to me any time you like in the evenings. I can talk to you about most subjects . . . but I am very immature about a lot of things that you, more worldly, people know. It's quite laughable really: at the Holy Office, as is well known, we deal with the problems and entanglements of love and marriage. Yet my knowledge is very limited. I've had to learn what little bit I do know the hard way!"

Cardinal Pacelli was crowned Pope Pius XII on March 12, 1939, and he spent most of the months that followed in trying to avert war and, once it had begun, to prevent its spread. But when Italy declared war on France on June 10, 1940, the sovereign Vatican State, just 108 acres in extent, was at once isolated in Rome. Pope Pius was determined to preserve the Vatican's neutrality and also to make it a refuge for as many as possible. Air-raid shelters were built, as well as steel vaults to hold some of the most valuable manuscripts and art treasures, a rigid blackout was enforced, and the diplomatic representatives accredited to the Vatican of those states at war with the Axis were brought into the Papal Hospice of Santa Marta, just inside the Vatican walls and at the rear of the Holy Office and the Collegio Teutonicum, which was later to prove extremely convenient for Monsignor O'Flaherty!

One of the first organizations to be set up by Pope Pius was a chain of agents throughout Europe to gather news of prisoners-of-war, refugees and the uncountable hordes of displaced and homeless, and it was decided that the Holy

Office, which under wartime conditions could not in fact carry out many of its normal functions, would centralize all the information and deal with POW and refugee problems generally. The vigorous O'Flaherty was selected to play a very special role. By the early part of 1941 there were tens of thousands of Allied prisoners-of-war in camps throughout northern Italy, and Pope Pius appointed as his nuncio, or messenger, to these camps Monsignor Bergoncini Duca with Monsignor O'Flaherty as his secretary and interpreter with British prisoners-of-war. They started out on their journeys at Easter 1941. Monsignor Duca set a sedate pace, visiting at best one camp a day; but this did not suit the energetic O'Flaherty, who had spent hours chatting to soldiers captured in Greece and Crete and during the first Axis successes in the Western Desert, sailors and airmen of the Mediterranean war, men whose families in very many cases could have no idea if they were alive or dead.

While the Nuncio stayed overnight as the guest of camp commandants or at hotels, O'Flaherty would make his way to the nearest railway station and rush back to Rome in the middle of the night so that the names of the POWs he had met and messages for their families could be transmitted over Vatican Radio at the earliest opportunity. Then he would hurry back again to join the Nuncio at the next camp. He was a true *Corriere di Dio* ("God's Traveller").

This work went on until Christmas 1942. In that time O'Flaherty *personally* collected and himself distributed to the camps more than ten thousand books and, true to the form he was to show later, blithely ignored "the usual channels", which of course included camp censors. Instead he enlisted the aid of priests in the countryside around the camps and issued the books through them, as well as a prayerbook which he compiled himself and had printed. He helped to speed

up the delivery of Red Cross parcels, slashing his way ruth-
lessly through Italian bureaucracy and tardiness, and above
all organized in his own mysterious fashion huge supplies
of winter clothing, something sadly lacking and badly needed
in the northern Italian winters.

So active was O'Flaherty, so heedless of protocol if it
stood in the way of charity, so blatant at evading regulations, that at last the Italian government decided it was time
this pest was kept out of their POW camps. "Representations" were made to the Vatican and, on instructions,
O'Flaherty resigned his position with his Nuncio—but not
before he had succeeded in getting two particularly bad camp
commandants fired from their comfortable jobs at Modena
and Piacenza.

Back full time at the Holy Office, the Monsignor soon
found himself busier than ever before. In November 1942
the Allies had invaded North Africa, and now the Holy
Office was dealing with thousands of inquiries from Italians
about missing husbands and sons, another army of POWs
to be traced and helped. As the war came nearer and nearer
to Rome, the Germans and Fascists stepped up their search
in the city for men and women they considered dangerous,
particularly prominent Jews and known anti-Fascists among
the Italian aristocracy. These were the very people O'Flaherty
had met at parties and, when they looked around for a place
of refuge, it was natural that they should seek out the
Monsignor at the Holy Office.

At the beginning O'Flaherty sent people who merely
wanted to go into hiding "in case" to reliable friends of his
in the city, in some cases to monasteries and convents; but
as tension grew in Rome, and more and more raids were
launched by the Fascists, he had to find other hiding places,
at least for some. With the audacity that was to be the

hallmark of his career from now on, O'Flaherty picked his own residence, the German College behind the Holy Office and also extraterritorial ground just outside the Vatican walls. The Collegio Teutonicum was not like the American, English, Irish or other training colleges in Rome. It was a place where for generations outstanding German scholars and church-men had gathered to live and study. There was a German Rector and the domestic staff consisted of German nuns. One or two Vatican officials had rooms here, including O'Flaherty, and among the people living there also by the summer of 1943 were the historian Hubert Jeding, Carl Testa, Jews, Austrians, Russians ... and a glamorous Italian princess.

Through all the years of Mussolini a considerable num-ber of noble Roman families had consistently refused to support Fascism in any way, and among these was the young Princess Nini Pallavicini, whose pilot husband was killed over Sicily. After the first two small air raids on Rome in July, the Fascists stepped up their searches for such people. Princess Nini had climbed out of a rear window of the Rospigliosi Palace near the Quirinale as a Fascist militia party burst through the front door. She made straight for St. Peter's, as so many were now to do, where she sent a message to O'Flaherty. From now on she was to become one of the Monsignor's most valuable helpers, particularly when it came to securing Italian identity documents and even escorting escapers into the Vatican itself.

By July there were seventy-four thousand known British POWs in Italy and with the fine weather more and more of them were escaping from camps or leaping from trains bound for Germany, and finding their way to Rome. Here they generally went first to the British Embassy in Via Venti Settembre, which was now partly occupied by the Foreign Interests Section of the Swiss Legation and under the care of a more-than-helpful Swiss named Secundo Constantini. Or they would go to the neutral Swiss Legation or to St. Peter's Basilica itself, claiming the ancient privilege of ecclesiastical asylum.

Of the thousand rooms in the Vatican, only some two hundred are normally occupied, residentially, by the Pope and his senior officials, and unknown numbers, particularly of Jews, succeeded in hiding safely in the City itself. Half a dozen or so Allied prisoners-of-war also got past the Swiss Guards and once inside were formally interned for the duration of the war. Very soon the Vatican Secretariat decided on stern measures and gave orders to the Swiss Guards accordingly. *All* who came asking to be interned were to be refused and, if necessary, forcibly expelled at the gates on each side of the Basilica.

The Swiss Guards, who were to play a considerable part in O'Flaherty's activities, are a remarkable body of men. Every one must be a native Swiss, Catholic, of legitimate birth and unmarried. They may not be over twenty-five years of age on first appointment, must be at least five feet eight inches in height and every one has the rank of Sergeant. After eighteen years a Swiss Guard can retire on half pay and the pension increases to full pay on retirement after thirty years. It is they who control all entrances and exits to the Vatican City and stand watch at the doors of the Papal apartments. Normally in blue, red and yellow uniforms, but in battle dress throughout the war, they are the military guardians of the Vatican State. The Palatine and Noble Guards have State duties, and police work is carried out by the Vatican Gendarmerie, all Italians of a minimum height of five feet nine inches.

The first group of fourteen British prisoners-of-war to be sent away from the gates by the Swiss Guards can be said to have started the Monsignor's real career as the Scarlet Pimpernel

of the Vatican. Standing forlornly and dangerously conspic-
uous in the vast St. Peter's Square, dressed in an assortment
of clothes they had acquired somehow, they simply did not
look like tourists or devout Catholics come to see the Pope.
One of the Irish priests who lived in St. Monica's Monastery opposite the Holy Office behind the Bernini Colonnade approached them and soon found out their predicament.
They were taken into St. Monica's for an hour or two while
O'Flaherty was consulted. True to his conviction that the
enemy rarely looks under his own nose, O'Flaherty hid this
first British group in an Italian police barracks, in the care of
a friendly carabiniere, where they stayed safely until the Germans occupied Rome on September 14, when the Italians
fled and all but one of the POWs were recaptured.

The Italian surrender on September 3, announced five
days later, and the military truce that began on September
11 started the floodtide of POWs. They poured out of camps
guarded by Italians who no longer wished to hold them;
those who had escaped earlier and hidden in the mountains
with peasants or the *partisani* now came out of hiding and
made for Rome. Quite a number of the escapers knew
O'Flaherty personally from his visits to their camps and went
straight to him; others were referred to him by the Swiss
caretaker Constantini; others were even put in touch with
him by the Swiss Guards.

At first O'Flaherty was able to send the men to personal
friends and the friends of friends, but by no means were all
of these friends rich, and food was costly and rationed.

Food and money had to be found, safe premises had to
be found, in fact a complete organization had to come into
being—just at the moment when the Germans were sweep-
ing into Rome to set up a stern military government and
the reign of the Gestapo.

CHAPTER THREE

The Council of Three

WITH HIS KNOWN and oft proclaimed dislike of the British, it was not strange that O'Flaherty had up to now had little or no contact with the one man who was very much concerned about this British "invasion"—Sir Francis Godolphin D'Arcy Osborne, British Minister to the Vatican, who with other anti-Axis diplomats was in the Hospice Santa Marta a hundred yards or so from the Collegio Teutoncium. Now the Monsignor walked out of the College, along the Via Teutonica, turning to the left by the great sacristy of St. Peter's, and entered the Hospice, built originally for pilgrims to Rome. On the ground floor were Vatican offices, on the first floor the Yugoslavian diplomats—men who hated the Germans above all else and seethed at their own incarceration; on the second floor was Mr. Harold Tittman, the United States Charge d'Affaires; the third floor held the French Legation to the Holy See and on the fourth and top floor was the British Legation.

The door was opened for O'Flaherty by a man who was every bit as remarkable as the visitor, a man who O'Flaherty himself said later was "indispensable, a genius, the most magnificent scrounger I have ever come across". The small man with the incongruous Cockney accent was John May, butler to Sir D'Arcy and surely the most unusual butler in diplomatic service. If O'Flaherty knew everybody in high society in Rome, John May knew everybody else, particularly "useful" people. Men who worked with the organization have said since that John May could work miracles! "You only had to ask him to find something and he would get it. He had the black market at his fingertips." May it was who knew, for example, exactly where fifty suits were being sold cheaply, where boots, cigarettes or razor blades could be found.

Sir D'Arcy Osborne was very much the old-style British diplomat, elegant, suave, reserved—even aloof, and certainly noncommittal. Told of the horde of British and other POWs rushing for Rome, he had to point out that he dared not compromise his position inside the neutral Vatican State. His work there lay in other directions. O'Flaherty's warm smile vanished, gone was the rather absentminded professorial look, his very blue eyes glittered angrily behind his spectacles and he told the Minister that *something* had to be done. "With winter coming on many will get sick, die even, if they are not sheltered. To give themselves up means a German prison camp and even worse conditions. You can't expect, Sir D'Arcy, that men who have had the courage and initiative to escape will tamely go back to their captors!"

The Minister smiled faintly at the storming Monsignor. Sir D'Arcy Osborne was often underrated—at first. Now within a few days of his fifty-ninth birthday, educated at Haileybury, British Minister at Washington from 1931 to 1935 and Minister to the Holy See from 1936, cousin and heir presumptive to the Duke of Leeds, he had his own ways of doing things, the devious ways of the professional diplomat, far removed from O'Flaherty's bull-like approach. Now he said, "You have, I believe, been helping some of these men yourself, finding money out of your own pocket for them. I will help you *personally* with funds as far as I am able, but I cannot use official funds, even if I could get enough, and I must not be seen to be doing anything to compromise the tacit conditions under which I am here in the Vatican State. What I suggest you do is to have a quiet chat with John May. I don't want to know any details, but I have a good idea he can help you!"

That evening, after the bachelor Minister had been served with his dinner and the butler was off duty, O'Flaherty and May met in the deep shadows on the top step of St. Peter's Basilica from where they could gaze down across the immense piazza to the white line painted by the Germans between the two arms of the towering Bernini Colonnade. On the far side of the white line stood heavily-armed German paratroops and generally there were also grim-faced SS men sitting waiting in a large black limousine. Rome was quiet now, outwardly quiet under the heels of the Nazis, peaceful after the battles of September 13 and 14, when the Germans had smashed their way through what Italian resistance was offered to occupy the Eternal City and ring it with tanks and guns.

"Look, Monsignor," said May, "this thing is too big for one man; you can't handle it alone ... and it's hardly begun! Oh, I know you've got every 'neutral' Irish priest in Rome helping you, everyone knows that. And there are the others, those Maltese, that big New Zealander, Father Sneddon, isn't it? Well, excuse me Monsignor, but they *are* only priests; I mean they don't know their way about like I do, and some of my ... er, friends! I suggest we have a sort of committee to take a bit of the burden off you—and you needn't tell Sir D'Arcy too much. As a start I'll see to the grub, and I suggest we get Count Salazar to help."

Thus was the Council of Three (later to become Four) set up. Count Sarsfield Salazar was in the Swiss Legation and

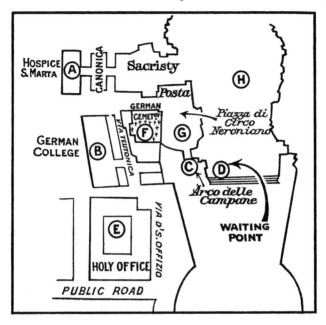

THE VATICAN AND ENVIRONS

This sketch map shows some of the key places in Monsignor O'Flaherty's adventures during 1943 and 1944. (A) the Hospice Santa Marta where the anti-Axis diplomats lived; (B) the German College where many escapers hid; (C) the Arco delle Campane and main entrance to Vatican City; (D) the point on St. Peter's steps where O'Flaherty stood waiting for anyone in trouble; (E) the Holy Office; (F) the German Cemetery, which, like the College and Holy Office, is on extraterritorial ground; (G) the Piazza di Circo Neroniano across which O'Flaherty smuggled escapers into the Vatican itself; (H) St. Peter's Basilica.

could pass on all requests for help made directly to the Legation or, clandestinely, through Secundo Constantini at the dust-sheeted British Embassy. If O'Flaherty loved plotting and May loved "fiddling", Count Salazar was the intriguer of all time! They made an astonishing trio. The major task was to find billets for the escapers and the first of these was provided by a magnificently heroic woman, Mrs. Henrietta Chevalier, widow of a Maltese who worked until his death shortly before the outbreak of war with a travel agency in Rome.

Mrs. Chevalier was left with six daughters and two sons but, as soon as Mussolini entered the war, the elder boy, Joe, was arrested by the Italians as a British subject and thrown into the Regina Coeli Prison, so grotesquely named after a church dedicated to the Queen of Heaven that used to stand near it. On a tiny pension Mrs. Chevalier kept her family in apartment nine on the third floor of a five-story block over shops, number 12, Via dell' Impero. In September 1943, Mrs. Chevalier was 42, Joe (now in a prison camp) was 23, Paul 22, Rosie 21, Gemma 20, Matilde 17, Mary 16, Anne Maria 13 and Henriette 9. (Henriette was to go and stay with Maltese nuns in Rome because she was too young to be kept in the apartment under the extraordinary circumstances that were to develop.) Mrs. Chevalier and the five remaining daughters shared two bedrooms, they had a dining room, kitchen, a tiny boxroom, bathroom with toilet, and another toilet on the back balcony. There was also a large larder.

Paul Chevalier had a clerical job, helping Constantini at the British Embassy, and was formally attached to the Swiss Legation staff; he lived there and had Swiss diplomatic papers. Early one morning a day or two after the Council of Three had established itself, Count Salazar contacted O'Flaherty. Two French soldiers had turned up at the British Embassy and been taken in by Constantini who was now awaiting instructions. O'Flaherty thought for a minute and said, "I'll send you a message in an hour, me boy." (Most people were "me boy" to the Irish Monsignor.) Leaving his desk and putting on his huge, flapping black hat, O'Flaherty set off with his giant strides into Rome to see which priest knew of a good hideout. He met a Maltese priest, Father Borg, and Father Borg naturally knew Mrs. Chevalier.

The telephone rang at lunchtime in the apartment at Via Dell' Impero and Rosie answered it. Cryptically Paul said only, "Rosie, tell mamma that I'm bringing home *two books*." He rang off. Putting down the telephone, Rosie repeated the message to her mother, who looked blankly at her. They had not the faintest idea what Paul meant.

In the late afternoon Paul turned up with the two French soldiers and the ever-cheerful, beaming Mrs. Chevalier promptly sat them down to a meal. Paul merely said, "Father Borg told me to bring them here. A Monsignor O'Flaherty is coming to see you tonight." By now Mrs. Chevalier guessed what was up, and when the family meal was finished and the dishes done, she turned to her two eldest daughters and said, "Take the young ones for a walk—all of you . . . out into the air! Go and see some friends . . . but not a word of any visitors here!" Excited and intrigued, the girls went off, and as soon as darkness came O'Flaherty arrived. Closetted with Paul and his mother, the tall Monsignor looked down at the five feet four inches of Henrietta Chevalier and said, "I must first tell you that all this is very dangerous. You do not have to do it. The Germans have said that they will execute anyone found harboring prisoners-of-war. But we must help these men if we can and you are the only one I can turn to tonight, for a day or two anyway. Say 'No' and I'll take them away now."

"What are you worrying about, Monsignor?" exclaimed Mrs. Chevalier. "God will protect us all, I know. I'm happy to help for as long as necessary. Anyway, they'll be company for the girls; we can do with a man or two in the house! We'll turn the dining room into a bedroom for them and we've enough bedding and mattresses, thank the Lord. I only hope we'll get enough food."

"I'll see to the food, somehow", said O'Flaherty. "Here is a little money to be going on with. Paul can let me know when you want more. Goodnight and God bless you."

Mrs. Chevalier had two mattresses on each of her divans and when the girls came back they had to take off two mattresses and make up beds on the floor of the dining room—a nightly routine to which they were to become very accustomed. For months from now on the Chevalier apartment was to be packed with escapers, once as many as nine sleeping in at the one time, on special occasions when acting as an emergency transit center providing food and shelter for a few hours for up to a score at a time! The Maltese nuns, who knew what was going on in Via dell' Impero, helped with food supplies from the convent garden. Mrs. Chevalier ("Mrs. M." was her code name in the organization that developed later) really did not fully appreciate the danger of her activities despite O'Flaherty's warnings, which he repeated every time he came. It was noted that the normally smiling Monsignor always looked grim and anxious when he visited the Chevalier apartment, never knowing quite what he would find. The girls, of course, thought it all great fun. The apartment was filled with the sound of "pop" music as the sisters danced with the soldiers endlessly to the gramophone—once work was done. Soon there were never fewer than four escapers hiding in the apartment. While Gemma worked as a cashier in a nearby furniture store, Rosie stayed at home to help her mother with the cooking and housework. The other girls were still at school.

Once the men had been issued false documents they could go out for exercise, but always escorted by one or more of the girls. Gemma was a great basketball player and towed her soldiers to the basketball stadium to watch her play. These outings were confined to the late afternoons—in the mornings the soldiers could rarely get out because they had to take their turn in the family queue for the bathroom, help replace the mattresses on the divans, and hide all evidence of their presence in the dining room ... and eventually in the boxroom also. In the beginning at least, if anyone was tense it was the escapers. From the day the first two Frenchmen arrived, Mrs. Chevalier rarely left her apartment but kept ceaseless watch over her "boys", constantly warning the girls against any indiscretion, presiding smilingly over her large "family". None of the Chevaliers' own friends were now permitted to visit them. The girls were not allowed to bring anyone home from work or school. Some of the neighbors in the block certainly knew what was going on, as did the block porter Egidio and his wife Elvira who organized a warning system later when raids were a constant threat.

Mrs. Chevalier, however, could not cope with an army of escapers and O'Flaherty decided that he would have to rent some accommodation of his own. Rome Radio was daily repeating the announcement of the death penalty for aiding escapers, and at this stage the organization was not developed enough nor were enough Italians willing to accept the risks they took later. The first of O'Flaherty's properties was typically located! A luxury apartment in the Via Firenze, the "Whitehall of Rome", just off the Via Nazionale, it was in a block backing onto the hotel which the German SS had commandeered as their headquarters and in the heart of the area under curfew and cordoned by SS guards. Another flat was rented in the smart Via Domenico Cellini in the Parioli district about a mile away.

To the Via Firenze apartment now went Lieutenant R. Wilson of the Royal Artillery, who already held the Distinguished Service Order medal for sabotage work behind the enemy lines. He had been landed by submarine to blow up some railway tracks and docks but failed to make rendezvous with the submarine that was to pick him up and so made his way to Rome instead. He presented himself at the Arco delle Campane, the arch under the clock on the left of the Basilica, and demanded to be interned. The Swiss Guards said, "Sorry, nothing doing." Wilson was not the man to take a refusal easily and protested so vehemently that two Guards picked him up bodily and dumped him in the center of the piazza, none too gently! For some reason the German sentries on the boundary line noticed nothing. Wilson picked himself up, stumbled up the steps to the Basilica and stood inside the biggest church in the world, leaning against a statue, bruised and very angry. He now had no idea what to do. For hours he stayed there until, just after dawn, the first Mass goers arrived. About half an hour later, as the steps were crowded with people coming and going, Wilson saw the tall figure of O'Flaherty beckoning to him.

"The Swiss Guards told me you've been here all night", said the Monsignor. "They have their duty, me boy, but you're all right now. Just follow me ... and don't talk!"

Wilson was taken by O'Flaherty in person to the Via Firenze apartment where he found some other British soldiers, a fiery Yugoslavian Communist named Bruno Buchner, who fretted at being hidden and wanted only to be out killing Germans, and a couple of Yugoslavian girls. Before O'Flaherty left, Wilson gave him a hastily-written letter addressed to the Pope himself, complaining of his "welcome" at the Vatican! Grinning, O'Flaherty took the letter and, undoubtedly with some satisfaction, handed it over to the Vatican Secretariat. Some days later he went back to the Via Firenze to give Wilson a reply from the Secretariat blandly inviting the officer to visit the Vatican at a more convenient time!

These apartments and the others that followed all cost money and so did the food. O'Flaherty's personal purse was not bottomless, though he never spent a penny on himself if he could avoid it, and Sir D'Arcy Osborne also had only limited funds. May had not yet perfected his techniques for money making on the black market, and the Monsignor was looking very worried one day, when the telephone rang.

"Filippo here, Hugh", said a voice. "I've been hearing some things about you! If you're short of money, as you must be, come and see me ... this afternoon if you can."

"Filippo" was Prince Filippo Doria Pamphili, head of one of the great Roman families noted for their anti-Fascist attitude. He was one of O'Flaherty's closest artistocratic friends and the Monsignor had often been to receptions in the eighteenth-century Palazzo Doria on the Via delle Corso, to which he now hurried.

"I think we will make sure of not being overheard, my friend", said Prince Filippo as he led O'Flaherty to the great picture gallery of the Palazzo. Standing in the center of the room, opposite the Velasquez painting of Pope Innocent X, considered to be one of the finest portraits in existence, watching that nobody came within earshot, Prince Filippo went on, "Even in my own Palazzo I am not safe from spies now! But my friends are telling me something of what you are doing, Hugh. Some who have been hiding escapers on their own tell me you have been giving them money, that they have only to appeal to you and help is always forthcoming. Here is 450,000 lire, all I can get my hands on today. Come back when you need more and I will do all I can. It is little enough."

Armed with this money O'Flaherty sat down at his desk and kept the Vatican switchboard busy with telephone calls to all the friends and contacts he could think of. All he wanted to ask—on the telephone at any rate—was if they had a spare room, a spare bed even? He rang round his duchesses and contessas, and the various colleges, monasteries and convents. May was doing much the same thing with his friends, though in most cases he had to visit his people, who either had no telephone or were far too cautious to talk on it these days. Everyone knew what the calls were really about. People were always to marvel at O'Flaherty's breathtaking audacity; he did not know the meaning of fear, genuinely caring nothing for the risks he himself ran. He took chances that really frightened his colleagues. For a long time he paid no regard whatever to the curfew if it prevented him from finding a new billet or escorting men there or going with money and food and any luxuries he could lay his hands on, such as cigarettes, fruit, razor blades and so on. As far as the Germans were concerned, he was to prove every bit as elusive a Pimpernel as Baroness Orczy's original hero.

CHAPTER FOUR

"I Want My Lucky Trousers Back!"

BY OCTOBER 1943, many hundreds of people in Rome knew pretty well what O'Flaherty was doing. The French, Polish, Yugoslavian and American diplomatic representatives all sought his assistance, and the Yugoslavians were particularly active because they had hundreds of *partisani* in the mountains who were in turn in touch with Italian peasants hiding escaped prisoners-of-war. One such was Lieutenant Colin Lesslie of the Irish Guards.

Captured in Tunisia on March 31, 1943, Lesslie was in Fontanello camp near Parma when his leg wounds turned septic, and on September 4 the Italians decided to move him to a hospital. He managed to jump out of the car and make his way up into the Appenines, where he found an empty cottage in which he hid for a day or two until the peasant who owned it turned up. The peasant, like many thousands of Italians who risked death in this way, told Lesslie to stay where he was and promised to help in every way possible.

Lesslie stayed in the cottage on a mountainside that was swarming with *partisani* until October 15, when the first snow fell in the area and it was clear that he would have to leave or die. Hundreds of men were in a similar position, and their trek to Rome and its environs was to stretch the O'Flaherty escape organization to the limit all through the winter. Lesslie's peasant friend took him, unshaven and in clothes that were mostly rags, to a nearby village and into the inn, which was crammed with *partisani* armed to the teeth. They were clearly waiting for someone and they took no notice of Lesslie, who sat quietly and a trifle uneasily in a corner. Then a chauffeur-driven Mercedes glided to a stop outside the inn and in came a tall, well-dressed and rather handsome man, carrying a bulging briefcase. His impeccable shave contrasted vividly with the bearded *partisani* who now clustered around him, each getting a bundle of money from the briefcase and then leaving separately. Alone at last in the room with Lesslie and his peasant friend, the man turned to the Lieutenant who had been covertly watching him all the time.

"I am told you are a British officer. Can I help you? My name is Cedo Ristic", he said with a flashing smile.

Lesslie explained that he needed respectable clothes and money for the train fare to Rome and from there on to rejoin the Allied lines. Ristic threw a frightening glare at the innkeeper who had chosen to appear from somewhere in the back and was now standing with ears cocked to hear every word. The innkeeper scuttled out to the rear again and Ristic said, "There is a problem. I do have some money left here in this bag but it is destined for two *partisani*. However, I have heard a rumor that they are dead, killed by the *Fascisti*, you understand? Tonight I will go and find out the truth. If they are alive then they must have the money and I cannot help you, at least not at once. But . . . if they are dead, why then the money is yours. We meet here tomorrow. . . ."

The next day the six-foot Irish Guards officer once more met Ristic in the village inn. This time the innkeeper stayed discreetly out of sight.

"They are dead!" reported Ristic. "So ... the money is yours. Here it is. One thing, though—in case you have any qualms of conscience, do not worry, forget them! There is nobody to whom you have to repay it, either. It is all forged lire, and very good too. It is *said* that it is printed inside the walls of Vatican City itself. I do not know ... I am not a Catholic ... I do not care!"

Lesslie bought himself a new suit and a train ticket for Rome. He was posing as a commercial traveller and with the nerve and same sense of bluff of the O'Flaherty he was soon to meet, he decided on the safest way to reach Rome. The Italians were looking for him but not the Germans. Passing down the train, he spotted a carriage in which were sitting five SS men. The Italians would never dream of looking for a fugitive sitting beside SS men, and as for the Germans, at that time they had nothing but contempt for all Italians because of the surrender. The Germans naturally assumed Lesslie to be an Italian and did not address a word to him throughout the journey. He arrived in Rome early on the morning of October 20 and reasoned that a church, any church, was the safest place to pause a while and think over the next move. All through the day he moved from church to church until darkness fell, and he then went to the office of the International Red Cross in Via Sardinia, where, he knew, Ristic worked for part of his time. Ristic was there.

"So! You have arrived safely. Good. Now what are you going to do, have you made any plans?" asked the Yugoslavian. Elated at having caught up with his friend, Lesslie burst out jokingly, "What's wrong with the British Embassy? If they've a room I'll stay there!"

"And so you shall!" Cedo Ristic roared, "So you shall! That is a first-class idea. It is all closed up and in the care of old Constantini, a sort of friend of mine, very definitely a helper, quite positively non-neutral for a Swiss! The Swiss are getting as useful as the Irish. These neutrals! I take you there now. . . . Come!"

It was one of the minor mysteries of the Rome escape story that for some reason the Germans kept no proper watch on the British Embassy, until the last few weeks. Possibly they simply could not imagine that escapers would dare to go to such an obvious place—though scores did—but, whatever the reason, it was not guarded as carefully as might have been expected, and it was fairly easy for Ristic to smuggle Lesslie into the embassy, where Constantini whipped the dust sheet off the Ambassador's bed so that the young Lieutenant could sleep in comfort for the first time in months. Lesslie spent about a week in the embassy and might well have hidden there indefinitely, until something made Constantini nervous and he contacted O'Flaherty. On the eighth or ninth night Constantini came to Lesslie and said, "You have a visitor, sir, in the drawing room!"

Downstairs, in the drawing room where gray dust sheets covered the chairs and sofas and the pale autumn sunlight fought to penetrate the unwashed windows, Lesslie met for the first time the Monsignor, taller than himself, beaming benevolently at him through his spectacles.

"Well, well, me boy, our first Irish Guardsman!" said O'Flaherty. "Now let us see what we can do for you." For a few moments he questioned Lesslie about his recent movements and then said, "Now, me boy, the British Minister to the Holy See wants to meet you and so does Mr. Tittman, the American Charge d'Affaires. I can't very well take you out of here in broad daylight but I'll be back—about eight o'clock."

Punctuality is not a virtue of the Irish but O'Flaherty was an exception. When he arrived he thrust a bundle of clothing at Lesslie. "We're near enough the same height", he said. "Here are trousers, shirt and so on." He dressed Lesslie in the full, red-trimmed robe of a Monsignor, complete with the distinctive hat. He himself wore a simple black cassock of the kind worn by an ordinary priest.

(When the war was over and Colin Lesslie was safely back in London, O'Flaherty wrote asking for his old gray flannel trousers back. He explained, "They are my lucky golf trousers and I don't like to play without them!" Unfortunately Mrs. Lesslie had given them away, but Lesslie sent a new pair—with the hope that the Monsignor would be able to play better than ever.)

O'Flaherty had a small black car at the back door of the embassy and swiftly drove Lesslie to the Piazza San Pietro and right up to the Arco delle Campane. "Now, me boy, we have a wee walk to take", said the Monsignor. "Ye're not to worry. I'll do all the talking. I'm going to be very vehement, d'ye see, with plenty of gestures and all that carryon, we're having a bit of an argument ... but you're not to answer back! Just keep nodding your head, very humbly ... so ... as if you were agreeing with me. That way we'll get by—please God!"

It worked. The Swiss Guards, who by now must have been acutely suspicious of *anyone* seen by night in the presence of the Pimpernel, came to attention and the two tall "clerics" passed under the arch. "Here, me boy," said O'Flaherty in comic imitation of a travel commentator, "is the site of Nero's Circus ... on your right St. Peter's itself ... just to the left there we see the German Cemetery ... ahead, right here, is the sacristy, and now you are across the boundary, in the Vatican City. This is the

Hospice Santa Marta—and some strange pilgrims it holds tonight!"

Introduced to Sir D'Arcy Osborne and sitting down with a large whisky and soda, feeling that life was suddenly very civilized once more, Lesslie chatted happily until Tittman arrived, when the two diplomats began to question him closely about conditions in the north of Italy and what was happening among the prisoners-of-war. When Lesslie had finished his account, Sir D'Arcy said reflectively, "Well, I really don't know, but it does seem to me as if the best interests of everyone would be served if all the POWs were to surrender. Winter is coming, is here indeed, and they can't survive in the mountains." He added, rather plaintively, "Besides the whole proceedings are acutely embarrassing for H.M. Government." O'Flaherty, who had been sitting back in his chair, staring at the ceiling and listening without interrupting to everything that was said, hauled himself abruptly to his full height.

"Sir D'Arcy," he said in an icily polite voice, "have you given any thought at all to what those men have gone through, their dreams of escape, the privations, the chance they see now of getting a step nearer home—indeed of getting back to their jobs and fighting some more? *Men's* dreams, Minister! How can you expect them even to consider the idea of giving up now?"

Tittman gave a dry cough and murmured, "Of course we are only too anxious to get as many of our men back Stateside as possible."

Sir D'Arcy looked around at the three men and said, "That is that then. Now, let us see what we can do about organizing things. Lieutenant Lesslie, if it can be arranged to have you interned inside the Vatican, would you like to stay on and help us all here with the work that has to be done?"

Lesslie thought swiftly. "Excuse me, sir," he said, "but can you, or perhaps the Monsignor here, tell me what will happen if . . . when . . . Rome falls to the Allies? What will be the attitude of the Pope then? As I understand the Geneva Convention, if I am interned in the Vatican I might have to stay here until Britain ceases to be at war with *any* state, and that would include Japan. Nobody knows how long that will take!"

Sir D'Arcy glanced at O'Flaherty, who replied, "I can give you no answer to that. I have no idea what the attitude of His Holiness would be."

"Nor I", added Sir D'Arcy.

"In that case," said Lesslie, draining his glass and rising to his feet, "I'll take my chance elsewhere, somehow. My first duty is to get back to my regiment."

"Oh, quite", agreed Sir D'Arcy.

"Sure, we get that", said Tittman.

"Come, me boy, it's time we ate", said O'Flaherty, and Lesslie followed him out, back across the Vatican boundary, down the Via Teutonica and into the Collegio. The meal was served in O'Flaherty's small and austere second-floor room, which held a desk, washbasin, sofa, two easy chairs and a radio. Part of the room was curtained off. The food was served on the desk by a German nun who smiled serenely at Lesslie's obvious confusion but showed not the slightest surprise at his presence. As the meal was ending, Lesslie noticed a bag of Bobby Jones golf clubs standing in a corner of the room.

"I've got some of those too", he said. "You are a keen player?"

That was quite enough to send O'Flaherty off and, for some hours, well into the night, the two big men played chip shots into the wastepaper basket. When both were too tired to play any more, Lesslie went to sleep on the sofa and the Monsignor retreated to the iron bedstead behind the curtain.

The next morning O'Flaherty took Lesslie to the apartment in Via Domenico Cellini. Here the only other resident on that day was the Yugoslavian Communist, Bruno Buchner, who had been shifted from the Via Firenze. Bruno was as fiery and as active as ever. Lesslie's sense of military security was outraged by Bruno's plain bravado. When, as the days passed, other British POWs arrived and feeding them became more of a problem, Bruno would go out as often as possible to collect Red Cross parcels. But these were distributed through the former American Embassy and right across the street from this building was a German barracks. Nevertheless, Bruno would walk coolly out of the embassy, arms laden with parcels, and saunter directly back to the apartment. It was, thought Lesslie, asking for trouble. Lesslie told O'Flaherty of his anxiety and the next night the Monsignor arrived to escort the Lieutenant to a new billet not far away. This had been found by one of O'Flaherty's legion of women helpers, the diminutive Miss Molly Stanley, who played a key role in the organization throughout.

Just after the end of World War I, when she was twenty, Molly Stanley had been sent to Italy to learn the language. She stayed for the rest of her life, as governess, secretary and teacher of Italian. Her role in the escape story began—as for so many others—with a mysterious telephone call one night late in September, soon after the German occupation of Rome. A woman who would say nothing about herself reported that two British soldiers were lying seriously wounded in a hospital taken over by the Germans, and were being refused the extra food they needed if they were to recover. First thing in the morning Molly Stanley—only five feet two inches, but *so* determined—strode into the hospital and had a talk with the ward sister, a Maltese nun. If, of course, the Germans had discovered that the little visitor was English, she would have been jailed instantly. Having learned that if extra food could be brought in, the nun would make sure the soldiers received it, Molly Stanley began daily visits with what supplies she could get. But her own money soon ran out and she sought O'Flaherty. For the next ten months O'Flaherty personally provided Molly Stanley with enough money for extra food and delicacies for her "boys", not only in the hospitals but in Regina Coeli itself. For soon Molly Stanley was going regularly in and out of the dreaded prison.

"Nobody bothered about such an insignificant little person as myself", she explained afterward. She would bring in food, cigarettes, birthday cakes (baked by the Duchess of Sermonetta for whom she worked at the time) and report to O'Flaherty on new arrivals. She would stand by, smiling calmly, as the guards cut her cakes into tiny pieces to see if they contained any secret messages. "As if I would do anything so silly, so obvious!" Day after day she visited the hospitals to check on the conditions of British soldiers and sometimes she got messages calling her to them. As on the occasion when the Maltese nun telephoned to say, "Please, Miss Stanley, come and deal with your two soldiers here. They are getting very much better—and chasing the nurses!" The governess who had disciplined two generations of Italian children came to the fore and little Molly Stanley left two grinning, but chastened, soldiers.

A day or two after O'Flaherty had moved Lesslie to his new billet, he visited him and said, "Things are getting rather warm, me boy. For your sake—and for the people here—I think we had better put you in the American College. You're too big to pass as an Italian, in fact you are too big to hide easily at all!"

The American College, unlike the Collegio Teutonicum, is a training center for priests of many nationalities and at this time it held a few Germans and some Japanese. Lesslie and all the men who were to be hidden there subsequently had to give their promises that, once inside the grounds, they would stay inside for good and never under any circumstances approach the College buildings themselves or any of the inmates, save one priest, Monsignor McGeogh, who would be their "contact". Lesslie found an assorted bunch of men in an old granary in a secluded part of the College grounds, from which the dome of St. Peter's could be seen a few hundred yards away. There were about fifteen American citizens of Italian extraction, mostly student doctors, who had been unable to get back to the United States after Pearl Harbor, eight British soldiers, one American GI, two American airmen, and an Italian air force pilot who had piloted Marshal Grazziani to the secret meeting with General Alexander, Commander-in-Chief, Allied Armies in Italy, which led to the Italian surrender. There were also a few elderly political refugees and a South African Protestant pastor, the Reverend Gordon Wiles. As he was taking Lesslie to the American College, O'Flaherty explained the rules and added, "You're in charge there. In places like this we always need a bit of discipline, and who better to enforce it than an Irish Guards officer!"

CHAPTER FIVE

The Coal Man and the Gestapo

WHEN O'FLAHERTY had told Lesslie "things are getting a bit warm", he did not bother to mention that he himself had just had an uncomfortable taste of how hot they were to get. Prince Filippo Doria Pamphili's first gift, substantial as it was, had not lasted long since, apart from the men coming into Rome, Count Salazar's "country branch" had to pay for the keep of hundreds, and later thousands, in the countryside—men who had been stopped from entering the capital and were hiding with peasants. It was time for another visit to the Palazzo Doria on the Via delle Corso. Colonel Herbert Kappler, chief of the SS in Rome, however, by now had a very good idea of the scope of the Monsignor's activities. All he needed was to catch him in the act. Kappler knew also that Prince Filippo would do anything to thwart the German occupying forces *and* was a close friend of O'Flaherty. A continuous watch was therefore kept on the Palazzo Doria. The SS men were instructed to stop nobody from entering but to report to Kappler personally if O'Flaherty was seen.

After this incident even O'Flaherty was to be more cautious about what he did in daylight, but on this brilliant sunny morning he raced at his usual gigantic pace down along the Corso Vittorio Emanuele, turned left up the Via delle Corso and bounded up the flights of white marble stairs to the third floor of the Palazzo where Prince Filippo, his secretary and a wealthy Roman friend were waiting. For some minutes they discussed money and where more could be secured. "Here is 300,000 lire (about £1,000) to be going on with and we are organizing a little collection among our friends—your friends. There's nothing to worry about, we won't let you down", said Prince Filippo.

"Oh, yes, there is something to worry about", cut in the secretary, who had been glancing out of the window down at the busy Corso. "Look here . . ."

The three men stood looking down. On each side of the Palazzo the street had been completely blocked by SS troops and the now well-known and well-hated figure of Colonel Kappler himself could be seen getting out of his black sedan. At that moment a servant came panting into the room to report that the Germans had completely ringed the Palazzo and were thronging the courtyard to one side of the building.

"I'm afraid this is it, Hugh", said Prince Filippo quietly. "There is no point in resisting. There is no way to escape this time."

"Don't you believe it!" retorted O'Flaherty. "Give me that money . . . thanks . . . we'd better find some other place to meet next time! I mustn't compromise you. If the Germans don't find me here they can't prove I was here! I'll think of a new rendezvous . . . bye . . . God bless you."

O'Flaherty rushed out of the room and fairly flew down the staircase to the main hall where half a dozen of the Prince's servants were standing nervously as the SS men banged angrily on the door. "Don't open it for a bit longer", hissed O'Flaherty and dashed to the back of the hall where a narrow, steep stone staircase led down to the cellars. Deep beneath the Palazzo, O'Flaherty drew breath and began to think hard. He knew the Germans would take the place apart if necessary to find him and there were no secret rooms in the building, no possible places to hide. How could he get through the SS cordon? He walked cautiously along a passage leading to the cellars that were actually under the Palazzo courtyard and then stopped, ears cocked. He could just faintly hear the shouting of the German troops in the building above, but there was another, strange noise, like rocks rolling down a mountainside.

Ahead a patch of light spilled out from one of the cellars opening off the passage—daylight! O'Flaherty raced to the cellar and stopped dead at what he saw. Prince Filippo was getting in his winter fuel supply and coal was sliding down the side of a small hill, reaching up to an open trapdoor in the courtyard. O'Flaherty began to scramble up the hillock of shifting coal, expecting a sackful to come crashing down on him any moment. But when he reached the top and carefully stuck his head out for a second, he saw that two coal men were standing by their truck parked outside the courtyard gates, rather anxiously watching about a score of SS troops standing stiffly in two lines across the yard. Nobody was looking in his direction. Raising his head a little more O'Flaherty saw an empty coal sack lying on the ground, just within his grasp. He thrust out one of his long arms and gently drew the sack toward him until he could pull it down into the cellar.

Slithering back down the coal hill, he took off his black cassock and stuffed it into the sack, his hat followed, and so did some coal. His hands were now black enough. He rubbed coal dust into his face and hair, ripped his gray collarless shirt down to the waist and covered shirt and chest with dust, then began to climb back up to the trapdoor.

As he reached the top he heard a voice, a German voice, calling in bad Italian, "You men, hurry on with your work and get out of here!" One of the coal men shouldered a sack and started to walk toward the trapdoor while the other busied himself moving sacks from the front to the tailboard of the truck. O'Flaherty ducked down and waited till he saw the mouth of the coal sack poised above his head and then spoke in a piercing whisper.

"Hold it! Stay exactly as you are and listen ... I'm a priest ... the Gestapo are after me. Leave that sack on the side there and come down here a moment!"

He did not know how the coal men would react—except that precious few Italians would now do anything for the Germans if they could help it. There was a gasp of surprise from the coal man, a grunt as he dumped his sack by the trapdoor, and then the man dived almost headfirst, to land sprawling on the top of the heap, beside O'Flaherty. When he had recovered his breath he looked at the Monsignor and grinned. "A new assistant I have, eh?"

"There's no time to waste", said O'Flaherty. "I want you to stay here a minute or two, no more. As soon as I've gone through the gates you can come out and get on with the delivery."

"Right, Father", said the coalman. "But don't let Marco, my mate, see your face! He's so dumb he might give you away."

Shouldering his sack, O'Flaherty hefted himself out of the trapdoor and started to walk swiftly across the courtyard. The SS men stood in their lines between him and the gates with a narrow gap in their ranks where the genuine coal man had passed through. As O'Flaherty approached, the SS officer gestured to his men and they disdainfully widened the gap so that their uniforms might not be dirtied. It never occurred to the SS men to wonder why a coal man should be carrying a full sack *out!* O'Flaherty marched through the gates, round the truck, and stood for a moment by the driver's cab where Marco, standing on the tailboard, could not see him. After a second or two Marco jumped off the truck, took a sack of coal, and started on his way to the trapdoor. The SS men were now all staring up to the roof of the Palazzo where other troops were searching and did not notice the first coal man pop up quickly through the trapdoor and start back across the courtyard with his empty sack.

O'Flaherty hurried round a corner. The narrow street in which he found himself was empty—all the Italians had cleared out of the way of the SS men. Quickly he emptied his coal sack, tucked his robes and hat under his arm, and dashed for the nearest church. Inside he startled the sacristan who was tending flowers on the altar and now gaped at the wild, filthy figure hurrying up the aisle. O'Flaherty genuflected before the altar and then said softly, "I need a wash, Brother." The sacristan wordlessly led him into the vestry and within minutes Monsignor O'Flaherty emerged once more on the streets, robed, hatted and recognizably himself again. He wasted no time in getting back to the Holy Office, but he did wait several hours before picking up the telephone. Prince Filippo himself answered, cautiously.

"I'm back home", said O'Flaherty softly. "Are you well, me boy?"

"Fine, now", replied Prince Filippo. "Some day you must tell me how you did it! I'm afraid Colonel Kappler is a very angry man. He spent two hours here, and he did say that if I *happened* to see you I was to say that one of these days he will be entertaining you in Via Tasso!"

For a while O'Flaherty lay relatively low. The Germans had settled firmly in control of the Eternal City. It was best if people came to the Monsignor, rather than he go to them, and nobody impressed this more on O'Flaherty than May, who was by now far more fond than scared of the Monsignor, and who told him bluntly, "You are a fool to expose yourself to unnecessary risks. You are too important. What *you* need is a sense of discipline! You stay at St. Peter's and I'll do the running about." As an Englishman, May himself would have been arrested at once if caught outside Vatican territory, but this never seemed to worry him and certainly never deterred him.

Night after night now, O'Flaherty stood on the topmost of the 22 steps of the Basilica, gazing out at the shadow-filled piazza, 1,000 feet long and 750 feet wide between the Bernini Colonnades—284 columns, each 64 feet high, in two double rows so far apart that two cars can drive abreast between them, and surmounted by 140 ten-foot statues of saints and founders of religious orders. In the moonlight 46-foot-high plumes of water waved in the breeze, soaring up from the two fountains in the piazza, and in the silence of the blacked-out city, if German patrols were not thundering through the streets on surprise raids, the murmur of the water "sounded like a mysterious call", wrote O'Flaherty in his guidebook to Rome. In black from head to foot, immobile for hours, plotting and praying by turns, O'Flaherty waited for those who needed him. From their station at the Arco delle Campane a few yards from him, the Swiss Guards on duty would smile knowingly. They were always ready to help, up to a point. May had a very special relationship with them, probably he "organized" supplies and facilities that were not normally available in the Vatican at that time, anyway the guards were generally in his debt and rarely refused to reciprocate if the butler did not ask too much. The Swiss Guards watched O'Flaherty for another reason. By now everyone knew that if the Germans could only lay hands on the Monsignor that probably would be the last anyone would ever see of him. The SS men and the paratroopers stared balefully at him night after night . . . but they could not cross the dotted white line to grab him. May and the Swiss Guards strongly suspected that O'Flaherty rather hoped the Germans *would* try, when he would be able to engage in a bit of boxing once more!

To O'Flaherty one night came Molly Stanley, imperturbably defying the curfew. At the top of the steps she went over to the rather sinister figure looming out of the darkness. O'Flaherty greeted her as ever with his enormous grin. Molly reported that one of the Monsignor's earliest and staunchest helpers, Prince Carracula, had been denounced to Kappler, who planned to raid his house that night.

"Right, Molly", said O'Flaherty. "Go on home now and get some rest. The Prince will be all right. We'll get him in here—somehow!" As Molly trotted into St. Peter's to pray that the Monsignor was right, he hurried down to the Arco delle Campane, collecting a salute from the Guards, and across to the Hospice Santa Marta.

"John," he said in the hall of the British Minister's apartments, as Sir D'Arcy Osborne passed by, pretending not to notice the visit, "can you borrow a Swiss Guards' uniform—at once?"

"I really do not see why not, Monsignor. Where do you want it?"

"Wait for me in the doorway of St. Monica's," said O'Flaherty, "and now I must hurry." He returned across the Piazza di Circo Neroniani and through a side door into the Holy Office, then through one of the three front doors and across the road to St. Monica's Monastery. Here he found an Irish priest and sent him to Prince Carracula's home.

"Tell him to come here with you right now. You have about an hour if our information is correct."

Within the hour Prince Carracula was peeling off his suit in the hallway of St. Monica's, while May, valet as well as butler, stood by to help him into a Swiss Guard's uniform. Now the Prince and O'Flaherty went to stand under the darkest part of the colonnade, while May scuttled back to the British Legation to wait nervously for the return of the uniform. As the clock struck midnight five Swiss Guards, led by an officer, came marching through the Arco delle Campane to relieve their colleagues in the piazza itself. They marched past the two men toward the watching Germans, then round the piazza, changed places with the off-going sentries and then these started on the return journey. "Go!" said O'Flaherty urgently as the small column drew level with them and Prince Carracula stepped smartly into line to form a seventh man. The Swiss Guards officer stared stonily ahead as he halted his men briefly outside the German Cemetery inside the gate, and Prince Carracula slipped silently across to the Collegio Teutonicum where a smiling O'Flaherty stood in the doorway with the Prince's own clothes over his arm.

Monsignor O'Flaherty, of course, had all his normal work at the Holy Office to carry out, apart from about two hours' devotions every day, and May kept much of the daylight watch in St. Peter's Square. One of the escaped POWs who had not been stopped and told to stay in the countryside was Corporal Geoffrey Power of the Royal Army Service Corps. He had heard about O'Flaherty and decided to make his way to Rome. He got a lift in a farm cart bringing the dawn supplies into the city and, after a rather awed glance around the vast Basilica, nervously went to the Swiss Guards at the Arco delle Campane. Almost before he had opened his mouth they told him, very firmly, to make himself scarce, and one Guard looked significantly across the piazza to the German patrol line, which was about to be changed for the day watch. Power started to retreat back across the almost empty piazza, without the faintest idea of what to do or where to go, when suddenly he heard a strong Cockney voice call out, "Hey, you there! Not so fast! Come back here!" Power turned to see the slight, natty figure of May in his short black jacket and gray trousers, stiff white collar and black tie, standing halfway down the Basilica steps.

"Well, well," said May, "a little lost lamb! We're used to them here. Now stay put. Don't worry about those layabouts over there ...", he gestured rudely toward the Germans. "They can't hurt you now. Just wait a jiffy. . . ."

In five minutes May was back with O'Flaherty, who took Power to his room in the Collegio Teutonicum, arranged for some food to be sent in to him, and apologized for the fact that he had to leave him for the rest of the day to get on with some work. "We'll fix you up tonight", he added. Power was taken for a few days to the Via Domenico Cellini apartment, where he met the bloodthirsty Bruno Buchner, but was moved to another billet before the fatal raid on this apartment.

By now a considerable change was coming over Monsignor O'Flaherty. In the first years of the war he was bluntly outspoken about his anti-English views. "I read the propaganda on both sides," he would say, "and I don't believe much of it. I don't think there is anything to choose between Britain and Germany." It was in the weeks immediately following the Nazi occupation of Rome that O'Flaherty's views underwent a drastic turnabout. Within days of their arrival, the Germans started to round up as many as possible of the hundreds of Jews living in Rome. Many of these had fled from the Reich as soon as Hitler came to power, some were retired professional people, quite a number were O'Flaherty's personal friends. Scores of Jews managed to get into the Vatican (the College of Cardinals was crammed with them), others O'Flaherty hid in his growing network of apartments and other hideouts, including his own old college, the Propaganda Fide, some he helped to leave the country.

One Jew made his way to St. Peter's and, coming up to O'Flaherty at his usual post on the steps and drawing him deeper into the shadows, proceeded to unwind a solid gold chain that went twice round his waist. "My wife and I expect to be arrested at any moment", said the Jew. "We have no way of escaping. When we are taken to Germany we shall die. But we have a small son, he is only seven and too young to die in a Nazi gas chamber. Please take this chain and take the boy for us, too. Each link of this chain will keep him alive for a month. Will you at least save him?"

"Of course," said O'Flaherty, "but I have a better plan. I will put the boy somewhere safe and I will look after the chain for you. I will not use it unless I have to. I will get you and your wife new papers, Italian papers, and you can continue to live openly in Rome." O'Flaherty was as good as his word. From the stock of forged papers and genuine, stolen ones acquired by Princess Pallavicini or manufactured by May (who was a very good photographer among his other accomplishments), or perhaps from the mysterious source inside the Vatican at which Ristic had hinted to Lesslie, papers were supplied, and father and mother survived the occupation and reclaimed their son at the end of the war.

At the same time O'Flaherty returned, intact, the gold chain. "I did not need it", he said simply. In fact he had tossed it into a drawer of his desk in the Collegio Teutonicum, where it lay month after month, rather to the apprehension of some of his helpers who, when they saw it, always urged him to put it in a safer place. "Why?" O'Flaherty would ask. "Nobody here will steal it."

On September 28, just two weeks after their entry, the Nazis demanded two million pounds in ransom for the lives of the Jews of Rome, threatening to arrest every single one and take them to Germany if the enormous sum was not paid—in gold. The Chief Rabbi of Rome, Dr. Zolli, went straight to Pius XII. Within twenty-four hours the money was raised by the noble families of Rome with the assistance of the Pope, who contributed one hundred pounds weight of gold by having some of the Vatican's sacred vessels melted down. At the end of the war Chief Rabbi Zolli, who had himself been hidden in the Vatican, became a Catholic.

The ransom did not, however, satisfy the Germans, and when O'Flaherty saw Jews being herded into cattle trucks and train cars—"these gentle people being treated like beasts", he said—he came to realize he had been wrong about some Allied propaganda at least. "I see now", he said as openly as he had expressed the other views, "that the Nazis are no better than beasts themselves, and the sooner they are defeated the better!" So far as their occupation of Italy was concerned, the worst thing the Germans could have done was start this persecution of the Jews. The average Italian, more than most races a mixture of openheartedness and materialism, was outraged by the whole ghastly performance, and O'Flaherty found he was beginning to get help from people who had hitherto stayed on the fringe because the Germans had done nothing to them personally. O'Flaherty could hardly bring more enthusiasm, more dedication to his task, conceived as it was as a work of pure Christian charity, but now with him and many Italians there was a much greater element of toughness, a straightforward anti-German attitude. Even the most conservative men in the Vatican were prepared now to give the trouble-shooting Irish Monsignor quite a bit more rope—provided he did not go too far. Pope Pius, who *did* know in outline about the activities, continued to turn a Nelsonian blind eye to the figure on St. Peter's steps, a figure he could see from his own study window as well as anyone else.

The Germans themselves helped harden O'Flaherty by their rather desperate attempts to capture him. From the day he took over in Rome, Colonel Kappler tried to plant spies and informers inside O'Flaherty's organization. The SS man knew quite well that the Monsignor lived in the Collegio Teutonicum, but he never managed to persuade anyone there to inform on O'Flaherty. Some informers were certainly located among the Italians inside the Vatican, and all the time Kappler was also trying to infiltrate his men into the ranks of the escapers themselves. There were times when he succeeded. O'Flaherty to the end horrified his associates by his utter trustfulness. It was not that he was a naïve man—he could see through sham as quickly as the next and he had no time whatever for poseurs. But when it came to spies he preferred to believe good of a man or woman until the opposite was proved, and even then was quicker to forgive than to seek revenge.

Until the organization took more formal shape under British military control, to a large extent there was no real security except what May, a thoroughgoing cynic if ever there was one, managed to ensure. May visited O'Flaherty in his room at the Collegio Teutonicum one evening and produced irrefutable proof that a particular "escaper" was a

German agent. O'Flaherty was silent for a while until May went on, "If I get the chance, I'll shoot the bastard ... begging your pardon, Monsignor!"

O'Flaherty rose from behind his desk, pulled back the curtain that hid his bed, and from beneath the bed tugged out a suitcase. Opening this, he showed the startled May a pistol and a box of ammunition. Coiled up beside the gun was a length of rope.

"If you shoot that lad, I'll shoot *you*, John", said O'Flaherty in what he thought was a convincing tone. "You don't have to worry about me, you see I've got my way of escape all ready, even if they come here for me!"

As May said afterward, "I don't think he even knew how to load the pistol, much less pull the trigger!"

CHAPTER SIX

A Repentant Judas

COLONEL KAPPLER now thought up another trick, a way to lure O'Flaherty down off St. Peter's steps and over the white line that protected him. Kappler had caught an Italian peasant, one of the men who daily drove into Rome with supplies for the markets, often bringing an escaped POW with them and carrying back money and supplies for Count Salazar's "country branch". Few men could hold out long against the torturers at Kappler's headquarters on the Via Tasso, men who varied the most primitive persuasions with modern scientific refinements, and the peasant was soon a broken man. He was promised his life and freedom if he would lure O'Flaherty out of the Vatican State on the pretext that he wanted to lead the Monsignor to an escaper. The peasant sent a message to O'Flaherty at the Holy Office and was told to come to the steps the next morning. There in the pale yellow autumn sunshine O'Flaherty stood in his usual position.

The piazza was unusually deserted, even for eight A.M., and the Monsignor was able to pick out every movement as a big black Gestapo car, looking from the distance like a toy model, purred up to the white line painted between the arms of the Bernini Colonnade to take up its usual vigil. Watching also was May, standing in the gateway under the clock with three powerful Swiss Guards only too eager to tackle any Germans who might literally step over the line. There were three SS men inside the car and they stayed there but, May noticed, the engine was kept running. Now the figure of the Italian peasant was seen entering the square through the right-hand colonnade. Haltingly he started to walk across the square, head down, not looking at O'Flaherty, but casting an occasional glance over his shoulder at the waiting Germans.

About a third of the way across he stopped, raised his head and stared straight at the tall figure on the steps. O'Flaherty moved forward a little, out of the shadow into the sunlight. May and the Guards stiffened. A small stream of people began to trickle out of the Basilica after early Mass. The Italian turned to his left and walked back to the inner edge of the colonnade. Very slowly now, limping slightly, he began to walk round the piazza, gazing straight ahead of him until he came almost level with O'Flaherty, when he dropped his eyes once more and moved on, round, and round, twice, then a third and last time. O'Flaherty smiled benignly down at him. May whispered to the Guards, "Just what is going on? I thought this might be a trap, now I'm sure of it!"

On his last circuit the Italian did look up at O'Flaherty, a wordless message from a repentant Judas, and then as he reached the far left-hand wing of the colonnade he dashed through it and into a narrow side street by the Holy Office. The Gestapo car had been facing the right-hand side of the piazza and long before it could turn the Italian had vanished.

O'Flaherty started down the steps after the peasant, but at his elbow appeared an unusually ruffled May.

"No, Monsignor! I am sure it was a trap. He was sent here to lure you out."

"But he hasn't even tried it, man", replied O'Flaherty impatiently.

"Precisely, Monsignor! We may presume—and hope—he has had a change of heart. Since the Germans will shoot him now if they get their hands on him again, I suggest that I go and hide him for a few hours and fix him up some place tonight. Perhaps you would like to go back to your office . . . and stay quietly there for a while?"

These were the sort of occasions, getting all too frequent as Kappler laid on the pressure, when John May wondered just how long the "wild Irishman" (as he called him behind his back) could last. As May once confided to Sir D'Arcy Osborne, "Sir, what the Monsignor needs is someone to run this setup for him. He's just too *innocent* for his own good!"

A few days later the very man turned up: Major Sam Derry.

Born in Newark, Notts, in 1914, Sam Derry grew to be six feet three inches tall and the only man in the Rome organization who could out-top O'Flaherty, albeit by a mere inch. A Territorial officer in the Royal Artillery, he was in France within days of the outbreak of war in 1939, survived Dunkirk to fight in the brief Syrian campaign, and then became a battery commander with the First Field Regiment, one of the Desert Rats, through 1941, until in July 1942, he was captured on the retreat to the last-ditch line at El Alamein. He found himself in the enormous prison camp of Chieti, the largest of its kind in Italy, holding twelve hundred officers. Here in due course he graduated to become a member of the Escape Committee, a distinct honor among a group of men of brilliant ingenuity. He had been a member only for a short time when early in 1943 the Italians in one swoop transferred most of the senior officers and all principal members of the Escape Committee. The Senior British Officer left in the camp at once appointed Derry to head the committee, and his first job was to try to find out who had disclosed membership of the committee to the Italians—something they could hardly have found out unaided. Derry personally suspected the small, swarthy Joe Pollak, a Cypriot of Czech extraction, who mixed little with the other prisoners but was always seen in animated conversation with the guards. However, there was no proof.

When the Germans occupied Rome, they also took over Chieti Camp, among many others, and broke it up, sending eight hundred or so men directly to Germany and many others, including Derry, to Sulmona Camp, an obvious staging point for the journey northward to the Reich. Within a short time the POWs were on a train bound for Germany, but Derry jumped off it, in a fashion that should have killed him, hid with peasants for a night, and on waking next morning, looked out across the countryside and saw in the distance the glittering majestic dome of St. Peter's. He was but fifteen miles from Rome.

Derry was ready to set off to walk to Rome, just like that, when the farmer and his wife in whose house he had spent the night managed to make him understand that there were other British prisoners-of-war hiding a couple of miles away, and they supplied a couple of giggling, excited boys, aged respectively eleven and thirteen, to take him to his compatriots. This group of men had simply walked out of their prison camp when the Italian camp guards fled. They were living now in caves and being fed by local peasants. They planned, it seemed, to wait for the Allied advance to overtake them and free them to get back to their own units and fight once more. Major Derry was not so sure. The men were in rags and, as he saw it, there was little likelihood that the Allies would reach them before winter set in. Derry was the only officer these men had seen since their escape, and he knew that it was up to him to do something for them. He went back to spend the night with his farmer friend and returned the following day to find that the number of freed POWs had doubled. Within three days he was in command of about fifty British soldiers 120 miles behind enemy lines. The objective was to get them back to the units. Money was the first necessity.

Derry knew that there were some British diplomats inside the Vatican and they were the obvious people to ask for money—or so he thought. He contacted the village priest, who understood English, and asked him to arrange for the delivery of a message to "anyone British in the Vatican". The priest gave him a quizzical look and agreed. The message said that a group of escaped Allied prisoners needed money and clothing and it was signed simply "S.I. Derry, Major".

This message was, like others, taken straight to O'Flaherty, who seized upon it eagerly when he saw it was signed by a major. The first thing he did was to send off three thousand lire, which would go a long way in the country, and that evening he took Derry's letter to Sir D'Arcy Osborne. The Minister shared O'Flaherty's view that it was high time there was some senior British officer in the Vatican, not only to help the Monsignor but to bring Service discipline to the mounting numbers of escaped prisoners; but he was infinitely more cautious than O'Flaherty could ever be. "Let us see what happens to the money," suggested Sir D'Arcy, "and then perhaps you can bring him to Rome and we can have a talk with him."

The priest who had arranged for Derry's message to reach O'Flaherty and brought back the cash had asked for a receipt for it, and Derry gave him a letter expressing thanks for the money—and asking for more if possible! This letter the priest undertook to take to the Vatican in person and when O'Flaherty saw the request for more, he turned to May who was in his room at the time and said, "This is the boy for us, John. He's got a bit of drive! Send him four thousand lire and bring him here."

In the chilly dawn of October 25, Derry was picked up by a cheery, bucolic smallholder named Pietro Fabri who drove regularly into Rome on his pony cart to deliver vegetables to the market. For a time Derry sat beside Pietro and one of the numerous Fabri daughters, Pietro occasionally bursting into song, Derry being more than slightly nervous, with the feeling that everyone was staring at him. On the outskirts of the city Derry hid under the mound of cabbages in the back of the cart while the party passed safely through a German checkpoint and, when they reached a marketplace, Pietro left his daughter in charge of the cart and took Derry to an apartment in a working-class tenement building nearby and handed him over to a small, middle-aged man dressed as a priest and named Pasqualino Perfetti. Derry took an instant dislike to him. He mistrusted him then and afterward.

When Pietro had gone off with a cheerful "*A presto*", Perfetti handed Derry over to another middle-aged man, this time in ordinary clothes. Aldo Zambardi spoke good English and said at once, "Now I have to take you to the Vatican. We will go by streetcar!"

Derry's glance down at his tattered shirt, battle-dress trousers dyed a streaky blue, and cut-down desert boots was enough for Zambardi, who found a pair of flannel trousers and a cloth cap and gave them to Derry together with his own overcoat. Zambardi warned Derry not to open his mouth and told him to pretend to doze on the streetcar, which rumbled across Rome to the Ponte Vittoria Emanuele, which the two men crossed on foot. They then walked boldly up the Via della Conciliazione to St. Peter's Square and there, standing on the Basilica steps with his hands folded in front of him and his head bent in prayer, was O'Flaherty.

Without a word Zambardi took Derry up to the Monsignor, who flashed him one smiling glance from his vivid blue eyes before turning on his heel, muttering, "Follow me, but keep a short distance behind." Derry was more than disconcerted to see that he was being led not, as he had anticipated, into the safety of the Vatican City, but through the colonnade and along a narrow street, then under an arch, across a square, and into a building over which was an inscription that could hardly reassure an English major—"Collegio Teutonicum". He had no idea who the tall priest was and strongly suspected the whole thing was a trap. There was, however, no alternative but to go along and see what happened.

O'Flaherty took Derry into a small waiting room, had a brief chat in Italian with Zambardi, and then turned to Derry, "Now we'll go up to my room, me boy. But first give Zambardi back his coat!" This done, Derry followed O'Flaherty up to the second floor of the building and into the small study-bedroom where Colin Lesslie had been only a few days earlier.

O'Flaherty did his best to put Derry at his ease, but the major was still quite apprehensive when the Monsignor sent him off to have a bath, handing him a bundle of clothes. Back from his bath, in the Monsignor's underclothes, his own shirt, Zambardi's trousers and O'Flaherty's very modish smoking jacket, Derry found the room empty and, after a precautionary peep behind the curtain across one end of the room, he was standing by the window, looking out across the German Cemetery and the buildings, squares and gardens of the Vatican City, when the door opened softly. Swinging round, still half-expecting to see the SS, Derry was nonetheless just as startled by a vision of the perfect English butler, smiling most winningly. It was, of course, John May, but he did not disclose his name. Instead he shook hands. "I thought you would be glad of these to celebrate your arrival, Major Derry", he said, and produced from a black briefcase a packet of cigarettes and a bottle of whisky.

May, who was always to prove every inch as cautious as Derry himself, asked a lot of questions but gave nothing except politely evasive replies to any that Derry put to him. When O'Flaherty appeared again he stayed only a second or two. "Ah, this is John May", he said, and bolted out of the room. May explained that the Right Reverend Monsignor Hugh O'Flaherty was an official of the Holy Office and people kept popping in to see him all day and half the night when they could. When Derry asked if the British Ambassador was in the Vatican, May explained that the British Minister to the Holy See was there, adding casually, "As a matter of fact I'm his butler . . . and I must be getting back to my duties."

Around midday O'Flaherty returned and lunch—bean soup and spaghetti, but a feast to Derry—was served at the Monsignor's desk by two of the German nuns. O'Flaherty explained that the College stood on extraterritorial ground and that Derry was safe enough in it even though practically everyone else there was German.

"All the same, we don't propose to tell them you are an English officer", he added with his huge grin.

After lunch O'Flaherty went back to his work—it was a Monday and the day on which the officials of the Holy Office prepared their documents for the Cardinals. Later in the afternoon he returned to the room. Derry was gazing pensively out of the window into the gathering gloom and did not hear the door open. He was consequently thoroughly surprised to hear in the Monsignor's rich brogue, "Blon, I thought you would like to meet this British major."

"Blon" turned out to be the extremely beautiful, nineteen-year-old daughter of the Irish Minister to the Holy See, Dr. Thomas Kiernan, a neutral to beat all neutrals ... and a man who was to be deliriously deluded by both his daughter and his wife who, before her marriage, was the world-famous soprano Delia Murphy, noted above all perhaps for her recording of the Irish ballad "The Spinning Wheel". After some casual chatter, which only left Derry more bewildered than before at the fantastic ménage in which he had landed, O'Flaherty and Blon went off, but a few minutes later in came May again, this time with an invitation for Derry and the Monsignor to dine with Sir D'Arcy Osborne that evening.

"What about getting into the Vatican though?" asked Derry, as O'Flaherty returned to the room after seeing Blon off. O'Flaherty said, "It's easy enough getting you *in*, but coming out again is another matter. We will have to think. . . ."

John May looked at the two tall men and said ingenuously, "It's surprising how alike you two are. . . ."

What Derry later described as a "cherubic smile" came over O'Flaherty's face and he said, "Yes, John, we'll be there."

CHAPTER SEVEN

The British Join In

THAT EVENING two identical figures emerged from the Holy Office and strolled toward the colonnade. Each wore the full formal dress of a monsignor, the low-crowned hat, long black cassock with scarlet buttons, scarlet sash, and silver-buckled black shoes. O'Flaherty had produced a duplicate of every item. He himself was the Scarlet Pimpernel of the Vatican literally as well as figuratively.

"Mind now," said O'Flaherty, "walk slowly, none of that parade ground strut! Keep your head bowed, and pray all the time. If you don't know any prayers, keep your lips moving anyway!" Derry prayed as he had never prayed before, the two men gliding with dignified pace past the Swiss Guards, across the Piazza di Circo Neroniani, past the Italian Gendarmerie, who took no notice of them, and so into the Hospice Santa Marta.

Thousands of men of many nations owe their safety to what went on at the dinner party that night, with the exquisitely courteous Minister presiding over a circular table set with softly-gleaming silver and glittering glassware, the guests in scarlet and black served with steak and mushrooms by an impeccable butler, who took each dish in turn from a liveried footman and listened unobtrusively to every word that was said. Derry, who had not had a proper meal for a year, was left in peace to deal with the steak, the grapefruit and the

cheese while Osborne and O'Flaherty chatted. Then, over
coffee in the drawing room, the Minister told Derry what
had been happening on the military and political fronts and
explained that Rome was now completely occupied by the
Germans, and that there were still quite a number of Italian
Fascists actively aiding the military government. In bits and
pieces Derry gathered some vague idea of the escape organization that was growing up around O'Flaherty. The three
men talked well into the night and then O'Flaherty left,
promising to return for Derry later that day. After he had
gone, Sir D'Arcy told Derry some of the almost incredible
story of the Monsignor's exploits to date . . . and at last came
to the point.

"We must appoint someone to coordinate all the work.
The Monsignor has decided you are just the man. Will you
do it?"

Derry consented at once, but said that he thought he
first should go back to his own group of escapers and make
some arrangements for them so that they would not feel
they had been deserted. The Minister agreed to arrange
this and May appeared, tireless, to escort Derry to bed. In
a few hours May woke him with a breakfast tray and, while
this was being disposed of, carefully laid out a selection of
the Minister's clothes that Derry would be able to wear:
shirts, socks, pullover, smart blue suit—and shoes from Berlin's
Unter den Linden! In the afternoon O'Flaherty returned
and Derry got back into the Monsignorial robes for the
walk back to the Collegio Teutonicum, a stroll he found
even more unnerving in broad daylight, with the line of
German paratroopers and the SS men linking the two arms
of the colonnade. Derry spent that night, the first of many,
on the sofa in O'Flaherty's room and was awakened at dawn
to be introduced to the shyly smiling Father Borg, the

Maltese priest who had arranged the Chevalier hideout. Father Borg took Derry back to Perfetti.

After he had changed back into the rags in which he had first arrived, Derry was escorted by Perfetti back to the market where Pietro Fabri was waiting, with a different daughter. Pietro motioned Derry to get up beside him and the cart jogged off. All the vegetables had been sold and Derry wondered how he would hide when they came to a German control point. He sat frozen as the guard signalled them to a halt, but the German only glanced into the empty back of the cart and waved them on. Derry learned later that while the Germans generally kept a rigid check on what and who went into the city, they rarely bothered about what and who came out, hence Fabri's nonchalance.

Halfway on the journey Fabri insisted on stopping at a wineshop. After the first round Derry had some anxious moments as he surreptitiously maneuvered in his trouser pocket to free a note from the bundle of fifty thousand lire Sir D'Arcy had given him. To produce the bundle in the wineshop would be asking for trouble. Even the thousand lire note he did hand to a delighted Fabri caused some curiosity, but it bought enough wine to make everyone unsuspicious and happy, and Fabri alternately chattered and sang his way home.

Derry made arrangements for his men, gave them money, and warned them to stay out of Rome and not to sleep in Italian homes even in the countryside, for if the escapers were caught it meant death for their Italian hosts. After promising to keep in touch and look after them, he returned to Rome under another pile of Fabri's cabbages. The routine was exactly the same and it all seemed much easier. On the afternoon of his return, wearing the Minister's expensive clothes, Derry sat in Sir D'Arcy's study for what he

hoped would be a full briefing on his duties. But Osborne
was in no hurry; gently, very politely, he asked question
after question about Derry's boyhood and background, the
best way to travel from Newark to London, and so forth,
and gradually Derry realized that he was being thoroughly
checked by a man less trusting than the Monsignor.

In fact the Minister had started his inquiries as soon as
Derry's name had first cropped up. Via the Foreign Office
and Scotland Yard, to Newark Borough Police Force, his
questions had gone and the police inspector who called on
Derry's father to tell him his son was alive and well, and
nothing more, gathered a great deal of information which
was relayed back to the Hospice Santa Marta. The Minister's
suave inquisition went on for quite some time, detail being
matched against detail, until eventually Sir D'Arcy smiled
his grave smile and said, "Right, I am satisfied." From then
on he was a different man toward Derry, he told him everything he could about the embryo organization and added
that in view of his diplomatic position, he himself could
not help directly or overtly, but he would be able now to
get some money from Britain. He suggested also that Derry
use some of the officers who were formally interned in the
Vatican as clerical staff, for there would be much paperwork, and documents would be far safer inside the Vatican
City than anywhere else. At that time already more than a
thousand escapers were in touch in one way or another
with O'Flaherty, but in most cases their names were not
known, and the first tasks were to get them all listed and to
inform their relatives.

The British escape organization that grew out of and operated side by side with O'Flaherty's activities came into being
on November 1, 1943. For the first few days Derry was
busy preparing a basic organizational plan, meeting the other

officers in the Vatican, and learning everything he could from O'Flaherty. The Monsignor and the Major had plenty of time to talk, for there was now a curfew, and they spent hours each night talking not only about business but on every subject under the sun. At the very start O'Flaherty said, "I know you are not a Catholic so we do not have to talk about religion, but I am very willing to talk about it any time you want." He was a brilliant conversationalist and, as Derry put it, "had the answers" to practically every question on controversial religious topics that Derry put to him. Although Derry wore the Monsignor's clothes to move between the Collegio Teutonicum and the Hospice Santa Marta, and the Germans in the College saw him in them and must have been perfectly well aware of exactly what was going on, nobody attempted to betray him or give any sign that anything unusual was happening. Later, as Derry and his helpers, and the scores of other Allied escapers living in Rome, moved, for a time, freely among the bars and hotels, the story was the same—not one Italian barman or hotel waiter ever informed on them—indeed they were the first to bring in warnings of any SS or Fascist Gestapo activities they heard about.

Very quickly Derry came to develop, like May, a great fondness for O'Flaherty and a remarkable respect for May, who not only had his own peculiar working agreement with the Swiss Guards, but freely and highly irregularly used the facility of his Minister's diplomatic bag out of the Legation to the Foreign Office in London whenever it suited him. Derry was told of Lesslie's incarceration in the American College and he asked May to go and see if the Irish Guards officer needed anything. Lesslie did want something. He knew that when first he was captured his wife, Eileen, had been visited by the village policeman in the middle of the night and told that her husband had been killed in action. In due course she learned that Colin was a POW, but when he escaped again, he was once more reported killed. How, asked Lesslie, was it possible to let her know he was alive and safe? May gave one of his appealing smiles and said, "Simple, sir. Just write me a check for a fiver on this piece of paper—I have a stamp. Here is the money, or I can spend it for you on anything you need. I will see that Mrs. Lesslie learns about you."

Slightly mystified, Lesslie did as May asked. After the war was over he learned what the wily butler had done. May had sent the check, with others no doubt, through the Minister's diplomatic bag to his own bank in Palmer's Green, London. Next Mrs. Lesslie got a bald message asking her to visit her bank manager, at Lloyds in Old Bond Street, where she was shown the check and at once, delightedly, identified the handwriting. Under a pledge of strict secrecy, the bank manager told Mrs. Lesslie that the bank had a good idea how the check had reached London and the circumstances indicated that somehow her husband was safe inside Vatican City. Later on, many British officers were to use May's unique banking facilities in this way.

In addition to the Council of Three—now Four with the addition of Derry—Captain Henry Judson Byrnes, a Royal Canadian Army Service Corps officer, and Sub-Lieutenant Roy Charlton Elliot, a young submarine officer, who were among those interned in the Vatican, started to tackle the accumulation of paperwork in the seclusion of the office vacated for them by the Secretary to the British Legation, Mr. Hugh Montgomery (now a priest). All important records, including receipts for money paid out, were buried each night in tin biscuit boxes in the Vatican gardens. Derry soon met many colorful characters, such as

Umberto Losena, former Major in the Italian Paratroop Corps, but now a British agent and the one man who could travel the country freely to gather information; Jean de Blesson and Francis de Vial, First and Second Secretaries at the French Embassy to Italy—where the Ambassador was a Vichy man and hand-in-glove with the Germans. Shocked at the bland way in which O'Flaherty introduced him to two men straight out of the enemy camp, Derry quickly discovered that the embassy was in fact nothing less than the under-cover headquarters of the Free French movement in Rome.

Derry was introduced to most of these people in the first few days before he started to move about Rome himself to a limited extent, in the small ground-floor room in the Holy Office where O'Flaherty normally worked. The Major had now been equipped with an identity document, no forgery this time, but a genuine Vatican pass, carrying Derry's own photograph (taken by May) and naming him as Patrick Derry of Dublin, a Writer in the Vatican service. And once he had this document, O'Flaherty and everyone else always referred to Derry not as "Sam" but "Patrick".

On December 8 "Patrick" received a considerable shock. He was already accustomed to O'Flaherty's habit of bringing in any and every odd character without the slightest check on their credentials or background, but almost always these people turned out to be safe, wanting either aid or an opportunity to help the organization. When, therefore, O'Flaherty telephoned across to his own study in the Collegio Teutonicum to ask Derry to come down and meet a visitor, the Major was prepared for almost anything. But not . . . Joe Pollak, the man he believed to have been the traitor of Chieti! If Derry's suspicions were true, O'Flaherty might have already given enough away to wreck the entire organization and ensure his own execution!

For some tense moments Derry chatted with Pollak, ostensibly casual, but in fact trying to find out what he had been up to. It was when Pollak said that he had reached Rome with six others and started to list them that Derry's heart lifted. For the first two names Pollak mentioned were those of Lieutenant Bill Simpson and Lieutenant John Furman, both Royal Artillery officers, who had been close friends of Derry's at Chieti. Both of them had escaped in daring fashions and linked up with Pollak. To test Pollak, Derry asked him to go back and bring Lieutenant Furman to the Vatican the next day. Sure enough, Pollak turned up with Furman and in style—the steel-nerved Cypriot having hired a *carozza* or horse carriage so that Furman could see something of the sights of Rome on the way in. Putting Pollak in a room on his own in the Collegio Teutonicum, Derry told Furman of his suspicions, but Furman said at once, "I think Joe Pollak is one of the most terrific chaps I have ever met!"

He explained that Pollak had on more than one occasion saved the lives of the whole party of six men and two Italian girls, Iride and Maria. Derry went back to the imperturbable Cypriot to apologize and explain his earlier cool attitude. Furman and Simpson, who were to become Derry's two chief assistants, were found a billet by the French Secretary, de Vial, after they had been fitted out with clothes from a relief organization run by Capuchin monks. Iride and Maria were sent back to the Sulmona area with money and supplies for POWs still in the district, and the other escapers were hidden in the American College. The next morning Simpson and Furman travelled to the Vatican by train and trolleybus to report for work at the Collegio Teutonicum.

Now, guided at different times by different people, Fathers Owen Sneddon, John Claffey, Vincent Treacy and Borg, or by Brother Pace of the De la Salle Order, sometimes with O'Flaherty himself, Derry visited the various billets, the private apartments, the hotel rooms, the warehouses, the monasteries—all the places where O'Flaherty had already concealed people. Simpson and Furman, now officially billeting officers, were themselves accommodated with two people who had helped O'Flaherty from the beginning, Renzo and Adrienne Lucidi. Renzo, a film director, was half-Danish and wholly anti-Fascist, Adrienne was one hundred percent French, and their home was the regular meeting place for many of the top anti-Fascists in Rome. Gradually Derry got a grip on the organization and issued code names—something the carefree Monsignor had never thought of. Here are some of them:

> "Mount"—Sir D'Arcy Osborne
> "Till"—Hugh Montgomery
> "Golf"—Monsignor O'Flaherty
> "Eyerish"—Father Claffey
> "Uncle Tom"—Father Lennan
> "Dutchpa"—Father Musters
> "M"—Mrs. Chevalier
> "Whitebows"—Brother Robert Pace
> "Grobb"—Father Borg
> "Sek"—Secundo Constantini
> "Spike"—Father John Buckley
> "Emma"—Count Sarsfield Salazar
> "Rinso"—Renzo Lucidi
> "Fanny"—Father Flanagan
> "Sailor"—Father Galea
> "Edmund"—Father Madden

The priests shared the really vital role in the organization: running supplies. With the money O'Flaherty had

received from his helpers such as Prince Filippo, and now
with the more orthodox and regular supplies from Sir D'Arcy
Osborne and British Intelligence, it was easy enough at this
stage to buy food on the black market (here May was in his
element). And Count Salazar's country organization had a
regular flow of carts travelling into Rome nightly with whatever food was available, not for the markets this time, but
for the escapers. Delivering the food to the scattered POWs
was a much more difficult matter. Each day one of the priests
took it in turn to load up a *carozza* and calmly drive it
himself out of the Vatican, past the German guards, and
then make the rounds from billet to billet. Father Galea,
for instance, would deliver to twenty-four hiding places every
time it was his turn.

Under the guidance of May, however, gradually most of
the *padrones* who were caring for escapers were introduced
directly to contacts on the black market, and life became
simpler when the organization was able to send money rather
than bulky supplies to most hideouts. Simpler in one way.
There was always the question of money. Derry recorded
that in the first six weeks of the organization's official existence, to December 9, 1943, he had distributed sixty-nine
thousand lire, but by the next four weeks more than a million lire had been paid out. Sir D'Arcy was handing over
one thousand pounds and more at a time, O'Flaherty continued to get financial help from those of his friends with
any money left, and the American Charge d'Affaires, Harold Rittman, was also helping to some extent. The trouble
with such American money as was provided was that it took
a great deal of pressure to get it out of Tittman at all, and
the number of United States servicemen now entering into
the escape line well outstripped the financial aid from their
own country. The United States officials tended to regard

the escape organization primarily as a sort of intelligence service, and wanted it to be used to send military reports out of Rome and back to the American forces to the south. Naturally, the British had from the start realized the secret service value of the organization, but they appreciated also that whatever was done in this line had to be achieved with the utmost tact and discretion to protect not only the neutrality of the Vatican and the position of O'Flaherty but the status of Sir D'Arcy Osborne himself.

The United States' approach was considerably more overt, and led to some coolness with their allies in Rome. Most of the American escapers were airmen who had bailed out of their bombers during operations over Italy. The British officers who were now administering the organization had three prime aims: to save escapers from recapture and imprisonment in Germany, possibly death; to inform the next-of-kin of the safety of the men; and to get every soldier, sailor and airman, especially those who could be the most useful to the war effort, back to their units and into active service again. All the men heading British escape organizations—in Italy, France, Spain, the Low Countries, even in Ireland— had the directive that, for example, flying crews were to be got back to work and fight as soon as possible. The Americans had a rule that if an escaped POW could be returned to his unit within twenty-eight days, he could then go straight back to combat duty more or less right away; but if this could not be achieved, the man had to be returned to the United States for six full months' leave. A number of the American airmen did not take at all kindly to some of the admittedly primitive billets provided in an emergency, or to the restrictions and disciplines that Derry tried to enforce on escapers who had reached Rome. "They expect, indeed they demand, to be put up in crack accommodation.

Anyone would think we were running five-star hotels", commented one billeting officer in a report to the organization. Quite a few of the airmen had no intention of missing their half a year "Stateside" and, even when it was possible to arrange to smuggle them out of Rome again and down south to their units, there was often difficulty in finding them—until the twenty-eighth day had gone past!

By operating between London and Rome through Switzerland, by financial stratagems that remain secret to this day, and in due course by working in such a big way on the money black market that they were able to make substantial profits on some currency dealings, the organization managed to find enough money for everyone, but only with the strict economy enforced by Derry, despite the rather pathetic pleas of his assistants from time to time to be a little bit more generous with "deserving cases". The standard daily allowance per escaper was initially 120 lire, which by then did not go far in Rome. But if one *padrone* was given a bigger allowance per man, others soon heard of it, and there was jealousy and trouble.

Money apart, the most constant need of the organization was boots, shoes, anything men could walk in. (In the height of summer 1944, Roman girls wore summer frocks and ski boots!) Most of the escapers had walked scores of miles and, even if they were only destined to stay in Rome, they had to have something to wear in the streets. For those who might have to make their way back to their units, footwear was even more important. May was generally able to get one or two pairs of boots from his friends among the Swiss Guards in a critical situation, but some bulk supplies were clearly desirable. May and O'Flaherty and the not-so-neutral ladies of the Irish Legation found an answer!

"Monsignor," said May one evening, as they stood on St. Peter's steps, keeping a watchful eye on the piazza for anyone who looked as if he might be an escaper, or anyone in distress for that matter, "Monsignor, I have made an interesting discovery. I really should have known this, but better late than never ... Do you know that the building that backs onto the garden of the Irish Legation has been taken over by the Wehrmacht—as a boot-repairing depot?"

O'Flaherty shot a quizzical look at the little butler. "That *is* interesting. I must pass the information on. Possibly something can be done. We might sow the seed of an idea."

Exactly how it was done they have never disclosed, but the boot depot was closed and unguarded by night—the thought of putting guards on a repair center of that kind never occurred to the Germans—and regularly for some weeks *someone* in the Irish Legation took quantities of boots from the depot, never too many at one time so that they would be missed ... and hurled them over the Vatican wall into a secluded part of the gardens, where they were collected.

Exactly what would have happened in Ireland if this exploit, and others yet to come, had become known to the Germans is a very open question. At that time the Irish Prime Minister, Mr. de Valera, was rigidly enforcing his policy of the strictest neutrality, at least at the political level. Be that as it may, it is a fact that while every German airman who parachuted to safety in Ireland was kept interned until the end of the war, dozens of British Royal Air Force officers and men, and later American Air Force personnel, including at least one U.S. general, were helped to get across the border into Northern Ireland, or over the Irish Sea to the coast of Wales, sometimes after a short token period of internment, sometimes within hours.

When the United States government, once it had troops in training in Northern Ireland, pressed Winston Churchill to occupy the whole country, and themselves infiltrated a number of Office of Strategic Services agents into the south—to the annoyance alike of the Irish and British Military Intelligence Services—Churchill, who openly criticized the Irish on many occasions (criticism that was positively welcomed by de Valera as underscoring Irish neutrality) replied to Roosevelt in a memorably terse note: "Leave the Irish alone. They are doing all right."

So they were—in Rome as well as in their own country. In one way or another about fifty Irish priests and theological students in Rome at the time were working for O'Flaherty.

CHAPTER EIGHT

Spies and Radio Romeos

O'FLAHERTY took a keen delight in the exploits of his associates. The innate fascination of a battle of wits with the Nazis and Fascists was now added to his unwavering determination to help anyone in trouble. Some aspects of this battle, however, created a very delicate problem for him. Quite naturally from their point of view, the British officers working with the Monsignor saw distinct advantages for the Allied cause in the intelligence and sabotage network that could be superimposed on the organization. Sir D'Arcy Osborne saw it too, indeed this aspect helped him get money from the Foreign Office, but he always affected total ignorance of any such activities. Nothing could compromise O'Flaherty more severely with the Vatican authorities than any suspicion that he was engaged, however indirectly, in espionage on behalf of the Allies. Yet, of course, he was indirectly involved right away, and later on was to take quite a positive hand in it. Derry, Simpson and Furman were now in touch with their own Forces.

Completely unaware of what was going on in Rome, the British Intelligence staff in the south of Italy sent an agent northward with money to help any escapers he might meet, to find out all he could, and plan to stir up any trouble for the enemy that proved feasible. The agent was an Italian, Peter Tumiati, who had for some years been a political prisoner of the Fascists. Naturally Tumiati knew O'Flaherty, as who didn't? And the first thing he did on arriving in Rome was to send a message to the Monsignor who sent for him and introduced him to Derry on the steps of St. Peter's. Derry was at first as reserved with Tumiati as Sir D'Arcy had been with him. How did the Monsignor *know* that Tumiati was in fact a British M.I.9 man? O'Flaherty was not to be drawn on this aspect but contented himself with saying, "I know him well." Derry decided to test Tumiati and asked him to get some street maps of Rome, badly needed by the organization. Tumiati procured these, and Derry then decided to send him back to Bari with a list of the two thousand or so escapers now being cared for by the organization in Rome and the surrounding countryside. How was Tumiati to get this sizeable list past any German examination? Found with it in his possession, he would be shot at once. The problem was discussed with O'Flaherty and May in the Monsignor's room in the Holy Office. For a moment or two after Derry raised the point there was silence, then O'Flaherty gave May a long hard look.

May actually so far forgot himself as to wink and then said, "I think we can arrange that, Major Derry. Just leave it to me. I will see you tonight."

That night May returned to meet Derry and Tumiati. "I've microfilmed the lot and they are in *this* one ... here." Handing over a few small baked rolls, he said to Tumiati, "Don't eat it!" Some weeks later Derry, listening to the B.B.C. broadcast from London on the radio set in the corner of O'Flaherty's study, heard the single agreed phrase that told him Tumiati had got through and the list was safely in London. By that time, incidentally, the list was well out-of-date and the number of escapers much greater.

Apart from Tumiati, Umberto Losena helped with arrangements for the Royal Air Force to drop supplies to escapers in the countryside and for the evacuation by troop landing craft of several hundred escapers concentrated near the Adriatic beaches. Losena was caught later on and put in Regina Coeli prison. Derry also had up to four secret radio operators working in Rome. A typical ruse was to transmit a message while sitting on a park bench, apparently cuddling a pretty Italian girl who would be, of course, part of the organization. The Free French, the Royal Yugoslavians (like Ristic) and the Yugoslavian Communists, the Greeks, the anti-Fascist noble Roman families and the Italian Communists were now all running underground movements and all becoming interlinked with the O'Flaherty organization.

So far as possible Derry tried to keep O'Flaherty in the dark about the intelligence and, later, sabotage work, but this was difficult as the Monsignor was no fool and in any event he was incorrigibly curious about the adventures of his friends. While insisting that he did not want to know anything he should not, he would always pop the disarming question . . . and had to be told the secret. In fact O'Flaherty got to know far more about British "cloak and dagger" operations than Sir D'Arcy, who was privately considered "too gentlemanly" to embarrass with any such information.

By now the division of duties at the head of the organization had been settled. Derry coordinated all activities as far as possible, O'Flaherty directed his small army of priests, monks and nuns who were responsible for finding new billets and getting supplies to them; Furman, Simpson and Joe Pollak took on the dangerous work of guiding escapers to the billets, issuing money (and getting official receipts for Captain Byrne's biscuit-box safes in the Vatican gardens) and helping also with the supply deliveries. To some extent

O'Flaherty worked on his own, helping all sorts of people in Rome, visiting hospitals and the Regina Coeli prison, going about openly by day and almost equally freely at night. He would often telephone Molly Stanley and ask her to meet him. He would then go striding off at his usual furious pace to some apartment or hideout with little Miss Stanley practically galloping in her efforts to keep up with him. There were two very good reasons why O'Flaherty chose Molly Stanley as his companion.

"When the Germans see a man and a girl walking along a street together they are usually not suspicious", he explained to her with a smile. "A man alone is far more likely to be stopped and questioned." He would always leave Molly waiting in a café or in a doorway where she could see him entering the building he had come to visit, and she had strict instructions to let Derry know at once if the Monsignor had been arrested.

The Germans were well aware that the British were somehow operating radio transmitters in the heart of Rome, and they were pretty sure one was working around Via dell' Impero, where the Chevaliers lived. (They were correct, but they never did find it!) One afternoon Paul Chevalier went to the apartment from the British Embassy and told his mother, "There is to be a sweep through all this area this evening." Immediately the apartment was filled with furious activity. The four soldiers currently in residence were set to work putting back on the divans the mattresses they had laid out for the night and were then sent off with Matilde, Mary and Anne Maria, the younger girls, at two-minute intervals, to meet in the next street and go for a long walk. Mrs. Chevalier whipped off the cloth and cutlery which Rosie had set on the kitchen table and then put just one plate and one spoon at each of six places on the bare table. "We are poor and we are crowded", she smiled at her two elder daughters. At 6.50 P.M. there was a discreet knock on the door, and when Mrs. Chevalier opened it the porter, Egidio, whispered hastily to her, "They will be here in ten minutes."

"We are ready for them", said Mrs. Chevalier and went back to the kitchen, picked up some sewing and sat placidly waiting for the Germans.

They arrived, as usual, with much thumping and crashing. As they could be heard working their way through the other apartments on the third floor, Paul opened the door to peer out, only to have it shut with a bang by an SS sentry standing outside. "Wait—we kom!" said the sentry grimly. Looking out of the kitchen window, Gemma gasped, and her mother, Rosie and Paul followed her pointing finger. Down in the central courtyard of the block the Germans had two trucks bristling with machine guns which were pointed up to cover the balconies at the rear of the apartments. There was to be no escape for anyone. Now there came the crash of a rifle butt on the front door of the apartment, and when Mrs. Chevalier opened it an SS trooper strode in, brushing her to one side, and stalked down the long corridor to the kitchen, where he placed himself by the door opening onto the back balcony. He was followed by a German officer with drawn pistol and four SS troopers.

At a gesture from the officer, the men began a careful search of each room, doing no damage but opening cases and boxes, missing nothing. The officer took one look at Paul as he entered the kitchen and snapped, "Your papers!" Wooden-faced, he knew better than to smile, Paul handed over his Swiss Legation pass. The officer grunted, handed it back, and turned to Mrs. Chevalier.

"How many of you live here?" he asked, and his eyes swept the table.

"Six, as you can see", replied Mrs. Chevalier calmly. (Afterward Gemma swore her mother had been enjoying herself at the German's expense.) "There is my son, Paul here", she went on. "But he lives at the Legation. My five daughters and myself, we live here."

The troopers began coming back from their search, entering the kitchen one at a time, giving a negative shake of the head, and then waiting quietly enough in the corridor. The officer idly picked up one of the gramophone records piled in one corner and Gemma stiffened in horror. Somewhere in that pile was a British disc which one of the soldiers had picked up somehow. If the SS man should see that ... but after a moment he began to walk down the corridor. With a gesture he sent his men out of the front door and then turned to Mrs. Chevalier with a smile on his handsome face.

"*Brava*", he said, with a half-salute, and closed the door gently behind him.

"What did he mean by that?" asked Mrs. Chevalier, back at her sewing in the kitchen once more.

"Do you know, mamma," said Rosie, "I think he was congratulating you on outwitting him somehow!"

The family nevertheless waited uneasily for an hour before the Germans had finished their comb-out of Via dell' Impero, and then Gemma went to a nearby square where her sisters and the soldiers would be watching out for her. When she arrived, the three young girls started straight back to the apartment together, the four soldiers returned one by one at intervals so that no watcher should see a number of men entering the block at the same time, and Gemma followed last of all, when she was satisfied nobody had noticed

anything. By 9 P.M. the whole group was having supper—
off a properly-laid table.

In the middle of this there came another tap at the door.
The soldiers looked in consternation at Mrs. Chevalier. The
nerves of everyone, except the remarkable "Mrs. M" were
somewhat frayed by now. True, the mattresses were not laid
out because it had been decided over the meal never in
future to prepare the beds until the very last moment, but
there was simply no way at all of getting out of the apartment if the Germans were back.

"It is only a little tap", said Rosie. "Not the Nazi way of
doing things. I'll go, mamma . . ."

She was back in a moment, smiling broadly. "It was only
Milko. He wanted to make sure everyone was all right."
One of the soldiers looked questioningly at Mrs. Chevalier.

"Milko? Sounds like a cow! Who is he, mum, and does
he know *we're* here?"

All the soldiers billetted with the Chevaliers were always
warned by Derry that they had two duties: the first was
never to compromise the family, to risk their own lives
instantly to get clear, rather than involve Mrs. Chevalier,
who would most certainly be executed, and to protect her
from any indiscretions which a woman unused to the circumstances of the times might commit.

"He's safe", replied Mrs. Chevalier soothingly. "He is a
medical student, poor as the rest of them, and he has a
room across the hall. He is safe all right—in fact he is wanted
himself by the Germans, or he would be if they had any
idea he was in Rome!"

Milko Scofic, a Yugoslavian, was studying medicine at
Rome University when the Germans first entered Italy. Just
as Joe Chevalier had been arrested and sent to a concentration camp, Milko found himself in a slave-labor gang in

Serbia. But the camp was overrun by Mihajlović *partisani* and he made his way to Ljubljana where he was reunited with his two brothers. They secured forged papers for him and he finally reached Rome once more where his uncle, Archbishop of Trieste until deposed by Mussolini, was able to help him rejoin the University with "Stateless Person" papers. Now he was twenty-five and with a considerable medical "practice" in the O'Flaherty organization.

At the time even Rosie and Gemma did not know what their mother was up to on the rare occasions when she announced that she was going for a walk or to visit friends. Sometimes she herself escorted escapers across Rome; more often she would take "Dr. Milko" with her to some man who was sick or injured, and a sitting target for any German raid, since generally he could not be moved. It was a bitter winter in Rome that year and the escapers, many of them underfed for months, succumbed easily to infections of every kind. Mrs. Chevalier had done a little nursing in a Maltese hospital in the First World War, now she had a regular routine for her sick calls. She would leave her apartment, cross the landing and tap four times on Milko's door. Usually he had his little black bag ready in his hand as he opened the door to the signal. As a precaution, Mrs. Chevalier would give him the name of a street in case they got separated, but never more than that at this stage. What a man did not know he could not disclose under torture, and Mrs. Chevalier was far, far more security-minded than Monsignor O'Flaherty!

She would not even leave the building with Milko. He would run down the stairs, she would descend in the rather creaky elevator. They would separately board the "*Circolare Rossa*", the streetcar that went round and round the outer suburbs of Rome, and sit in separate seats but within sight of each other. Sometimes, if she felt uneasy, Mrs. Chevalier would stay on the streetcar for three or even four circuits of the city to make sure they were not being trailed before rising to get off, followed by Milko.

On other occasions that winter it was Milko who crossed the hall to tend patients in Mrs. Chevalier's dining room. Ronald Wenn and Pat Flynn, two Territorials who had been caught trying to leave Tobruk on a raft and had subsequently escaped from Bari prison, were lodged by O'Flaherty with Mrs. Chevalier for some time. Wenn fell ill with a temperature of 103°F, and "Doctor Milko" and Mrs. Chevalier nursed him back to health. Wenn and Flynn were out walking with two of the Chevalier girls one afternoon when a small, tubby priest was seen walking toward them. The priest hesitated, slowed his pace, and smiled directly at them as he passed by. "*Buon giorno*", he said, then walked placidly on.

"Who was that?" asked one of the girls and Wenn replied slowly, "I think ... I'm almost certain ... that it's Geordie, a Glasgow lad who was captured at Tobruk with us!" (It was. Wenn and Flynn were to meet him again, at Gestapo headquarters.)

There were five British soldiers in the apartment, including Wenn and Flynn, for the next German raid on the building. This time it was Elvira, the porter's wife, who gave the alarm. Milko had pressed the button to call up the elevator on his way to his studies at the University when Elvira almost fell out of it. "They're just coming in!" she said and raced across the hall to warn the Chevaliers. Milko shut the elevator gate and saw the elevator start to descend. He ran down the stairs and out into the central courtyard. On this occasion the SS men had no machine gun watch in the yard and he was able to wait there. The whole raiding party went upstairs and Milko was able to get clean away. It was his room the Germans wanted to search!

In the Chevalier apartment there had, of course, been no time for the five soldiers to get away and, bearing O'Flaherty's instructions in mind, they rushed out to the balcony and let themselves down over the side, hanging on desperately to the railings and praying that no Germans would enter the courtyard, look up and see them. The SS men combed Milko's room but found nothing suspicious, made a perfunctory search in another apartment, and departed without ever going near the Chevaliers!

That evening O'Flaherty turned up at the apartment, looking harassed and, for him, quite stern-faced. The British soldiers had gone out for some fresh air with Rosie, Anne Maria and Matilde, leaving Gemma and Mary with their mother. The latest raid had been reported to O'Flaherty, who wanted to know if Mrs. Chevalier felt unable to continue. Once again he impressed the danger on her (something she was beginning to appreciate now), but she pleaded with him to let her keep her "boys". Shaking his head doubtfully, O'Flaherty gave in—people generally did give in to "Mrs. M". The Monsignor turned to Gemma and Mary and groped in his cassock, finally producing two tickets for the Rome Opera House.

"Have you ever seen *The Barber of Seville?*" he asked.

"Never", said Gemma. "The opera house is far too expensive for us."

"Well then," O'Flaherty thrust the tickets at her, "you can go tonight, if you hurry. These tickets were bought for two British officers who are great opera lovers. (They were in fact Simpson and Furman.) But there have been rather too many visits to the opera house by escapers lately, and the Germans plan to raid it tonight and catch anyone they

The door of St. Monica's Monastery, in the shadow of the
Bernini Colonnade, where so often O'Flaherty arranged
for escapers to change clothes.

ABOVE LEFT: Colin Lesslie dressed in Msgr. O'Flaherty's robes, in which he was smuggled into the Vatican. ABOVE RIGHT: Colin Lesslie, London film producer, 1958. BOTTOM LEFT: Butler-extraordinary and superb scrounger, John May. BOTTOM RIGHT: Sam Derry.

The military men of the escape organization. *From left to right*: Lieutenant Furman, Major Derry, Captain Byrnes, and Lieutenant Simpson.

The identity card forged in the Vatican for Sam Derry.

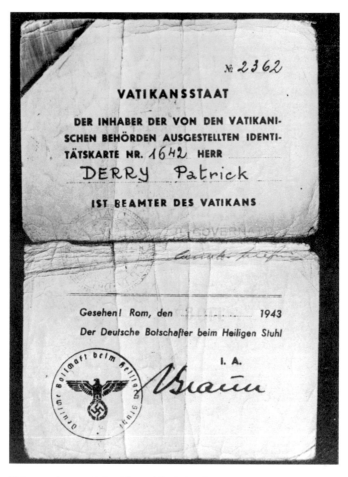

This was the pass John May tricked the German Minister into issuing
to Sam Derry.

Tiny Molly Stanley, visitor to the dreaded Regina Coeli prison.

Maltese heroine, Mrs. Henrietta Chevalier.

Msgr. O'Flaherty with Mrs. Chevalier (in white hat) and her daughter, Gemma, and Cpl. Kenneth Sands, just after Monsignor had married Gemma and Kenneth.

ABOVE: Msgr. Hugh O'Flaherty, Col. Sam Derry and Eamonn Andrews after the BBC's *This Is Your Life* program, which told Derry's story on February 19, 1963. BELOW: Twenty years after it all began, two tall men tower over this group seen in the program—O'Flaherty and Derry. Beside "the Pimpernel" stand Cameron Highlander and Norman Anderson. To the left of Derry in the foreground are his sons Andrew, James, Richard and William. Mrs. Nancy Derry holds daughter Fleur Louise. Everyone else in the picture was either a member of the rescue organization or an escaper. On the extreme right is Michael Denison and beside him Captain "Pip" Gardner, V.C.

can. Sure, it's a great pity to waste the money—they're the best seats, too—and you can have a good laugh at the Germans!"

Indeed opera-going was a favorite recreation with many of the escapers. Milko got hold of six tickets one day and took five of O'Flaherty's escapers with him, to seats right in the middle of a group of SS officers. Not one of the escapers except Milko could speak Italian (and he was just beginning to learn his English from the Britons). But they stuck it out and got safely back to their billets.

Lieutenants Simpson and Furman, who were now living with Renzo and Adrienne Lucidi, went frequently to the opera and on one occasion came out with what could have been a priceless memento. They were sharing the Lucidi box, with the beautiful Adrienne on the right-hand side. The soprano was Maria Caniglia. A second or two before the curtain rose, the box on the right was occupied by a heavily-decorated German general and half a dozen or more of his staff. During the first intermission Renzo and the two British officers were highly amused to see the admiring glances that the general was casting at Adrienne. As the curtain was falling for the second intermission, Renzo leaned across Simpson and Furman to whisper to his wife, "If he likes you so much, ask him for his autograph!"

A mischievous smile lit up Adrienne's face and as all the lights went fully on she caught the general staring hard at her while his entourage continued to gaze stiffly to the front. She leaned over the side of the box and thrust her program under the nose of the German officer nearest her.

"Would the general honor me with his autograph?" she asked softly, but loud enough for him to hear. The officer was clearly about to refuse indignantly when the general half-rose in his seat to face Adrienne and said, "Most

certainly, Signora. It is I who am honoured!" And taking
the program he signed it across one corner and then handed
it back to the officer to pass to Adrienne, who could barely
succeed in hiding her giggles. The general and his aides
now stalked out of the box, presumably to the bar, and the
three men looked at the program as Adrienne held it out,
shaking with laughter.

"Well, I'll be damned!" said Simpson. "The new Military Governor of Rome no less! This could be *very* useful."

For the first few weeks of the occupation the Military
Governor had been the Catholic Austrian Air Force General Stahel but, probably on the advice of Colonel Kappler,
Hitler had decided that Stahel was too lenient and had
replaced him a few days before the opera incident with General Maeltzer, who had an eye for a pretty woman.

Simpson could hardly wait until the next day to show the
prize to Derry: the authentic signature of the virtual ruler of
Rome. It was rumored after the war that this signature was
the one which the O'Flaherty organization used for the forged
passes they turned out by the hundred. In fact Derry merely
kept the program safely in case the signature was ever needed
because O'Flaherty, with Princess Pallavicini and May, could
produce all the passes that were ever needed from the Vatican printing presses. Derry, Simpson and Furman actually
had *genuine* passes signed by the German Minister to the
Holy See, Baron von Weiszacker!

The Minister regularly issued passes to Vatican staff who
had to move about Rome after curfew, which had been
brought forward from 11.30 P.M. to 7 P.M., and one morning when the Vatican Home Affairs Secretariat had prepared a small pile of passes to be taken to Weiszacker for
signature, the ubiquitous May appeared in the Secretariat
offices on some errand or other. He returned to the offices

later that day, on some other excuse, and after having given Sir D'Arcy his after-dinner coffee, came grinning into O'Flaherty's study in the Collegio Teutonicum to hand Derry three signed passes.

Maeltzer wasted no time in "toughening up" conditions in Rome. Kappler was given more men and the Italian Fascists formed their own brand of Gestapo, under an Austrian named Ludwig Koch, which was in many ways even more dangerous and certainly more vicious than the SS. As Italians, the neo-Fascist Gestapo, as they were termed, could penetrate hideouts in city and countryside much more easily than the Germans, and they built up a lethal network of informers among Italians who saw no hope of an Allied advance in the winter and, resigning themselves to German occupation, found it expedient to work with the conquerors and their Fascist torturers and murderers. With this new manpower, the Germans were able to develop their own spy system enormously, and one plainclothes Fascist Gestapo man was posted more or less permanently opposite a tobacconist's shop in Via dell' Impero, from where he could watch the whole street. This shop, which was run by a middle-aged American woman, was the one patronized by the Chevaliers—until the day of Gemma's adventure.

Normally cigarettes, when available at all, were provided for the escapers by the priests, by O'Flaherty, Simpson or Furman on their rounds. On this particular afternoon, however, there were none in the apartment and Gemma offered to see if she could get some from the tobacconist. In the shop the American woman, who did not know for sure but like quite a few others in Via dell' Impero probably had a fair idea of what the Chevaliers were up to, thrust a large carton of cigarettes into Gemma's hands.

Gemma was about to express her thanks when something in the face of the American woman made her pause. She scrabbled in her handbag for more money, put some lire on the counter, and left the shop without another word. Across the road she saw an Italian man watching her. Instead of walking back up Via dell' Impero to the family apartment, she turned the other way. The man followed her, she could feel his eyes boring into her back, and suddenly she dashed down a narrow side street, clutching her carton of cigarettes. She heard the man's footsteps ringing out behind her as she emerged into a main street and dashed across the road—straight across the path of a streetcar. Amid shrieks from passersby, the Gestapo man put his hand across his eyes and only looked again when he heard the streetcar clattering on instead of grinding to a stop. The road was strewn with cigarettes, but Gemma had got well away.

She did not at first tell her mother of this occurrence, and for a while longer the Chevalier ménage carried gaily on as before.

CHAPTER NINE

Christmas—and the Fearful Days Begin

WITH CHRISTMAS drawing near, the escapers became exuberant. The officers, when they had money—either their allowances from Derry or from checks cashed by May—visited the best bars in Rome and ate in the best restaurants. The Fascist newspapers complained about this open defiance and Maeltzer closed some establishments, but this only made him more unpopular with his own officers, who lost the facilities also. The sheer nerve of the young Britons, South Africans and Australians was to cause a lot of worry for Derry and contribute materially to the Vatican's hardening attitude to O'Flaherty's entire operation. O'Flaherty himself, fun-loving, could see little harm in it all. "It keeps the boys happy and seems to annoy the Germans", he said to Derry one night. Derry was, however, gravely concerned not so much this time for the personal safety of the escapers, but that some indiscretion, some looseness of security, too much wine, a casual word, might lead the SS to any of the hideouts. The risk was ever present and, despite the fact that all the escapers were under orders not to go near their own hideout or any others of which they happened to know if they were being pursued or thought they were being followed, it did happen from time to time. One young officer, "Peter", very nearly betrayed the Lucidi's apartment in this way.

Peter had taken a very pretty young contessa out for the evening to the Casino della Rosa in Umberto Park, which was literally kept in business by the underground Allied and the German officers. He was grinning broadly as, having gathered his coat and hat from the men's cloakroom at the casino, he rejoined his contessa in the main hall. "What is so funny?" she asked. Strolling toward the streetcar stop, Peter told her, "You know it really was a great temptation. Kappler himself was there tonight, he often goes I gather, and of course even he has to leave his gun in the cloakroom. I don't know where the attendant was, but I had to get my coat myself, and there, hanging on the wall, was Kappler's darn great pistol. I nearly swiped it!"

The young officer's laugh and the contessa's delighted giggle both came to an abrupt stop. Just turning a corner ahead and about to face them were two of the Fascist Gestapo, swaggering bullies who were now even more hated than the Germans. Quick as a flash Peter thrust his contessa into a shop doorway.

"Stay there until I've got out of the way", he hissed and started to walk on up the street. He kept his eyes cast down but saw the Fascists give a hard stare as he passed. He was a few yards on and breathing more easily when the cry he dreaded came—"*Documenti!*" He stopped, walked back and showed his papers but something about them or perhaps Peter's own very non-Italian appearance, made the Fascists suspicious. Pulling their guns, they prodded him along the street toward their headquarters—and Peter knew very well what would happen to him there.

Swinging round, he knocked the gun from one Fascist's hand and tripped the other man, then ran. Shots whistled after him and people in the street fled into doorways for cover. Down one street and up another, doubling back on his tracks, he thought he had lost the Fascists when he came out into Via Scialoia, where he recognized the building in which Renzo and Adrienne Lucidi lived. He dashed into the hall and, fortunately for him since he did not know the number of the apartment, Adrienne herself was chatting with the porter. Taking one look at the young man, Adrienne guessed what was happening. With a meaningful glance at the porter, she grabbed Peter's sleeve and tugged him across to the elevator. They shot up to the top floor and then out onto the roof where Adrienne hid him in a large bin half full of sand.

Down in the hall the two Fascists came storming through the door. As he saw them coming, the porter put on an excited expression and didn't wait for the Gestapo men to speak but burst out, "You've just missed him ... he ran clean through to the back and out that way ... he's only gone a few seconds!" The Fascists charged through to the back of the block, out by the service entrance, and away down the street.

It was not only such incidents as this that kept Derry, Simpson and Furman busy trying to maintain some sense of discipline among the 160 or so men they had in the city itself at this time, but the eternal problem of money. There were constant requests from the *padrones* and from the escapers themselves for more cash. When the escapers met at the bars or anywhere else and got talking together, they quite naturally compared notes on their respective billets and exchanged stories about their landlords and landladies. Those who were billeted with the wealthier or more generous Italians, Maltese, or any other nationality, would boast of the "good grub" they received. Mrs. Chevalier's "boys" were notoriously well catered for. Her own daughters would complain, half jokingly, that their mother always regarded the men of the household as having priority when it came to feeding. Girls could take their chances, they needed less, she would say.

Coming up to Christmas Derry authorized an issue of another twenty lire a day for extra comforts—except for those staying with "Mrs. M", who were in no need of assistance! Here Gemma Chevalier kept the family accounts, in an old school exercise book she has to this day. She did most of the shopping also, and shopping for the "family" was a major chore. Gemma or one of the other sisters would leave the apartment at midnight, swathed in a blanket against the bitter cold, so as to be at the head of the queue for the butcher or the baker. All the shops they needed were in the Via dell' Impero and there was no doubt that most of the tradesmen had a very shrewd suspicion that the Chevalier family were feeding many more than themselves. But they were not betrayed.

The butcher, Giovanni Ceccarelli, was in the secret almost from the start, and he himself often brought a large supply of meat up to the Chevalier's apartment and handed it over to Simpson and Furman, who would then carry it round to the other billets at Via Domenico Cellini and Via Firenze. The amount of money handled by Mrs. Chevalier and the quantity of supplies that went through the apartment were quite considerable. Between November 7, 1943, and January 3, 1944, over five hundred pounds was spent and there was about one hundred pounds of food stored in the larder.

Most of the escapers, in Rome at least, managed to celebrate Christmas Day, 1943, in some fashion. Gemma's shopping list for December 23 read like this:

Bread	Kg. 16	L 405
Eggs	50	L 700
Meat	Kg. 14	L 1820
Turkeys	Kg. 16.50	L 1485
Xmas tip to porter		L 500
Salt	Kg. 13	L 1495
Tomato sauce	Kg. 10	L 850

And on Christmas Day she recorded the purchase of eight liters of wine for 192 lira. There is no record of the precise number of people in the apartment over Christmas, but it was packed throughout the day and most of the night as various priests in the organization called in. On January 6, Feast of the Epiphany, the accounts showed that no fewer than twenty-one people were fed; on January 8 the number was sixteen. These figures probably include men at the other two billets.

In many ways it was a depressing Christmas although everyone in the organization, from O'Flaherty to Molly Stanley, did what he could to make things cheerful for the escapers, most of whom had expected to be home long before this. Miss Stanley, with the help of other women, prepared a small Christmas gift for every single escaper in the care of the organization in Rome, now around 180 men. Each gift was accompanied by an English Christmas card.

The busiest man of all on Christmas Day itself was Monsignor O'Flaherty—the priest not the Pimpernel. First he said Midnight Mass for his group in the Collegio Teutonicum, which was attended by the non-Catholics as well, some of whom had never been at a Catholic service before, and then he walked up the hill to the American College to say Mass there in the old granary. The South African padre held a service for non-Catholics and then the men settled down to Christmas dinner, of spaghetti and rolls, reinforced for the occasion with some apples, chocolates and a few bottles of wine. Next O'Flaherty visited as many billets as possible before returning to the Collegio Teutonicum where he and Derry had their lunch—mutton—off a corner of his desk as usual, served by the silent German nuns. Through the afternoon and evening and through St. Stephen's Day the small room was crammed with visitors—the varied collection of people O'Flaherty had hidden in the College, priests of half a dozen different nationalities, the Irish Minister, Dr. Kiernan, his wife Delia and Blon and seventeen-year-old Orla, the fiery Yugoslavians, May, of course, and Sir D'Arcy Osborne, charming as ever and not blinking an eyelid at the people he saw there. Rigid abstainer though he was, O'Flaherty was always a more than generous host, and for some hours all were able to forget their cares and responsibilities to the accompaniment of Irish airs sung by Mrs. Kiernan, including the soft, delicate lullaby "The Spinning Wheel", and Father "Spike" Buckley's vastly more robust version of "Mother Machree".

They were the last hours free from grave worry that anyone connected with the organization was to have for months. From December 27 the fearful days began.

Kappler and Koch were tightening their grip on Rome, the 7 P.M. curfew made communication with the billets far more difficult and meant also that escapers often had to be taken across Rome in broad daylight instead of under the cover of darkness. This was dangerous under any circumstances but doubly so when the escapers were six-foot blonds or black Americans or flamingly red-haired Scots, none of whom could possibly pass as Italians. Then the Vatican authorities themselves, ever restless at O'Flaherty's activities, decided to stop at least one blatant practice and they

closed the front gate that led from the street into a courtyard beside the Holy Office and then to the Collegio Teutonicum. This meant that every visitor to O'Flaherty had
to pass through the heavily-guarded checkpoint at the Arco
delle Campane. May, however, dealt to some extent with
that problem in characteristic fashion. While it is true that
he could "charm the birds off the bushes" when he wished
to be persuasive, charm by itself was hardly likely to have
much effect on the Swiss Guards. Whatever May's hold on
the Guards or influence with the commander was, he managed to arrange for the use of the small guardroom inside
the arch where visitors could be met and their all-important
reports taken. Even so, Simpson, Furman and the priests
concerned with ration distribution had to cut their visits to
O'Flaherty to the minimum.

The next blow came when, owing to the imprudence of
some Allied escapers, of which there had been about six
hundred in the Arda valley alone, the police arrested eighteen Italians who had been helping the men, and the SS
and the Fascists were now directing all their efforts to locat-
ing the source of the money they now knew the escapers
had received. Of course this pointed directly at the Vatican.
Originally Derry had decided to evacuate the Via Firenze
and Via Domenico Cellini billets by December 31, but
delayed the order because of the difficulty of finding other
premises.

Disaster struck on January 5 but O'Flaherty and Derry
did not learn of it until the next day. On January 6 Simpson, Furman and Pollak all arrived together at the Arco
delle Campane, something most unwise except in the real
emergency this was. They were lucky. O'Flaherty was actually striding back from his lookout post on the Basilica
steps when he saw his three aides. He took them into the

guardroom and then, making sure the coast was clear, sent them one by one across the courtyard and up to his room where Derry greeted them in consternation. Nothing he had expected was as bad as the reality. For it looked now as if Iride, one of the Italian girls who had brought Simpson, Furman, Pollak and the others from Sulmona into Rome, was liable to betray them all, or had already done so. And Iride was one of the very few on the fringe of the organization who knew of "Patrick"—Derry—and of O'Flaherty's role!

True, Derry and his brother officers had been reserved in their attitude to Iride for some time. From the very start she had done wonderful work for the escapers, travelling regularly into Rome and returning with food and money from Derry. She seemed to be able to get away with whatever she liked, and when one day O'Flaherty made some casual reference to her achievements he went on, "I wonder just how she does it, nobody else could hoodwink the Germans as she does. She comes and goes half the time on German trucks and I can't imagine how she has deluded the drivers all this time."

Somewhat embarrassed, Derry said, "Well, Monsignor, she is a very attractive girl you know, even if a bit, er ... garish, and as a matter of fact she gets on very well with the German drivers. She ... ahem ... well she provides them with much-appreciated services that only a woman can give!" O'Flaherty shot a keen glance at a slightly pink Derry and paused while the soldier wondered just how the priest would take this revelation about one of his helpers. O'Flaherty said merely, "What a pity", and changed the subject.

What Derry did not tell O'Flaherty was that on her first visit to Rome on behalf of the organization she had lived—and sheltered some escapers—in perhaps the safest place of all, a brothel—the one place where a more or less constant procession of men in and out would attract little attention from the SS.

On the previous night, January 5, Furman and Renzo Lucidi, quite by chance, met in the street Henri Payonne, a French officer who had just returned with Iride from one of her trips to Sulmona. There was no time for a chat because the curfew was almost upon them and Furman gave Payonne the Lucidi's telephone number, asking him to ring up later that night, and warned him not to give the number to Iride or to anyone else as it was a standing precaution with the officers to try to ensure that as few people knew of the activities and locations of others as possible. No call came that night but early in the morning the telephone did ring and when Renzo answered, it was *Iride's* voice on the line! She asked to speak to "Giuseppe"—the name by which she had known Pollak at Sulmona—and then told him she must see him at once.

Pollak discussed the new situation with Simpson, Furman and Renzo Lucidi while Iride made two more calls, imploring Pollak to come to her. When the telephone rang for the fourth time Adrienne answered it. After a second or two she rushed into the room where the four worried men were discussing Iride and screamed, "Get out—they're coming here!" The fourth call had been from Payonne, who could only say that everyone was in danger. Within minutes Simpson, Furman and Pollak were out of the Lucidi's home. They hurried to the Via Domenico Cellini base where they left their luggage and made directly for the Vatican and O'Flaherty.

The Monsignor sat grim faced at his desk as he listened to the story. Pollak insisted that he ought to go to Iride and find out what was happening. Derry and O'Flaherty

were certain it was a trap. Eventually, having handed over
his documents and personal valuables, Pollak was permitted to go at noon, with the understanding that if the
Monsignor had not heard from him by three P.M. it would
be assumed that he had fallen into a trap. As an additional
precaution, it was arranged that a Yugoslavian girl named
Graziella would trail Pollak to report if anything went wrong.
May joined the group in O'Flaherty's room and the
Monsignor postponed some work at the Holy Office and
stayed sitting silently in a corner of the room. It was not
until four o'clock that the bell rang and O'Flaherty was
up and across the room to his desk in one huge stride.
After putting down the telephone he said, "That was
Aldo [the College porter]. A young Italian has a note for
'Patrick' and will give it to nobody else. It sounds like
another trap." O'Flaherty wanted to go down to the
lodge himself as Derry spoke no Italian anyway, but eventually Furman went and returned to the study with a note—
from Iride. Slowly Furman translated and read out the
letter:

"Dearest Patrick,
    "Yesterday at midday I was arrested and I got the news
that my mother, my sister and my baby, as well as Flora and
her family and the famous 'Dino', who knows Giuseppe,
had also been arrested and were in the hands of the German command. We were betrayed by Captain Dick . . . ,
who is not a Captain but a simple Medical Orderly, who
had divulged everything. They are here looking for Giuseppe
and at all costs must take him.
    "I begged Giuseppe to come to me because I am very
sick but I am guarded. I think that the arrest of Giuseppe
will be the saving of us all. I won't talk unless threatened
that I endanger the life of my baby by not doing so—in

which case I shall poison myself. I beg you however to save the lives of my baby and my poor mother.

"You must not believe that if they take Giuseppe that it is a betrayal—he is of no interest to them—they only want to know who supplies the money and I repeat they will never know from me—I prefer death—I am only afraid Giuseppe may talk if he believes himself betrayed.

Iride."

Joe Pollak was arrested by two SS men as he entered Iride's room at the boarding house she always used now in Rome and was at once taken back to Sulmona with Iride. There was nothing O'Flaherty or Derry could do for either of them at the moment and they concentrated on precautions in Rome. It was planned to move the twelve escapers in Via Domenico Cellini and put Simpson and Furman in for a few days until safer billets could be found for them.

But the next blow fell almost immediately, on January 8.

CHAPTER TEN

Escapes, Captures and Tortures

THOUGH DERRY did not know it at the time, many of the German raids throughout Rome during this period were not on account of the escape organization at all, but in search of Communists who were busy ambushing and killing any Germans on whom they could get their hands. Kappler now concocted a plan to trap as many as he could at one time. Two SS men visited a widow whose Communist son was in the Regina Coeli prison and told her that they had just been released from the jail where they had worked out a plan for the rescue of her son. He was going to pretend to break down under torture and offer to lead the SS to the hideout of his Communist friends. Now, if the widow could assemble her son's friends, *they* could ambush the SS men when they arrived and free the son. The widow took the two men along to Nebolante, a leader of the Italian underground— and also one of O'Flaherty's *padrones* who was at that very time sheltering Lieutenant Wilson (the man who complained to the Pope) and Captain "Pip" Gardner, V.C., M.C.

These two escapers uneasily shared the lunch Nebolante offered the SS men, who appeared to satisfy Nebolante that they were genuine. The two SS men left and Wilson and Gardner were about to start to lecture Nebolante on his trustfulness when the door burst open and uniformed SS men poured in. They took the two British officers and

Nebolante to Regina Coeli and left guards in the apartment with the cook, an old man who knew of the Via Firenze and Via Domenico Cellini billets and of the secret doorbell signal used by the escapers.

This Saturday was the day on which Simpson and Furman had arranged to clear the Via Domenico Cellini apartment and move in themselves. Simpson arrived first, to find an addition to the usual group of escapers—a man who claimed he was Adolf Hitler! This was an American Army Air Force Sergeant named Eaton who had injured his head when his aircraft crashed. He had been brought to the apartment by a South African named Burns who had been moved from it a few days earlier. Burns had now vanished. Eaton was holding an animated conference with the German General Staff, watched by an unsympathetic Bruno Buchner, who was in charge of the apartment at all times. Simpson telephoned for the Royal Army Medical Corps doctor, Captain Macauley, and when he arrived, left the apartment to see if O'Flaherty could get Eaton into a hospital, for a hospital he clearly needed. Practically on the doorstep he met Furman and explained the position. Furman said he would wait with Eaton until proper arrangements could be made. Eaton had occasional lucid moments but most of the next half hour, while Furman, Buchner and Macauley waited anxiously for Simpson to return, was spent listening to the American's sick ravings. Then the doorbell rang, and there was Nebolante's cook—with two SS men. Half a dozen more flooded into the apartment. In all, the SS arrested five officers, two privates, Eaton, Buchner and Herta (the Austrian girl who acted as housekeeper). On the way by truck to Regina Coeli, Furman, with astonishing coolness, managed to tear his identity documents and his notebook with the coded addresses and telephone numbers of the organization into tiny fragments and push the bits, a few at a time, out of the truck. He was left with twelve thousand lire and this, while waiting in a cell for interrogation, he stuffed into a bread roll he happened to have in his pocket. This money was to be used for buying black market American cigarettes and other little luxuries for the prisoners. In Regina Coeli, Furman learned, the Nebolante cook, who could hardly be blamed at his age for not standing up to the Gestapo, had led the Germans also to the Via Firenze apartment, where three South Africans were arrested. Furman was desperately worried that the Germans would now round up the whole organization and find their way straight to O'Flaherty and Derry. He was not to know of Simpson's adventures.

Simpson actually returned to the Via Domenico Cellini while the SS men were still inside the apartment. He gave the secret bell signal but it failed to work properly. One SS man did indeed hear something and went to the door. He was just opening it when Simpson caught sight of the Italian porter signalling at him frantically from down the corridor. As the SS man flung the door wide, Simpson raced up to the next landing and threw himself full-length to the floor. Through the bannister he watched the SS man impatiently test the bell and then go back into the apartment. When all was quiet again Simpson slipped out of the back entrance and reported the situation at once to Derry who, however, already knew of it because two British privates had been in the basement of the building when the raid was launched and they got out, raced to the Swiss Legation to send a message to O'Flaherty—and walked right into a police check as they left the building. They were arrested, but their message had got through.

Now O'Flaherty sat down at his desk and telephoned for hours, contacting every one of his priests to warn them of the position and also to get them to check on their billets so far as they dared. Derry was distinctly dubious about exposing the priests to such risks at this time but the Monsignor managed a faint smile as he said, "Sure, me boy, you have enough to worry about without that. Most of these billets are with private Italian families and it is quite normal for a priest to drop in on them, d'ye see. Even if the Germans are watching some places they'll think nothing at all of a priest going in."

"But", protested Derry, "we must assume that a large number of billets are being watched, though I agree I might be looking too much on the black side. And if the Germans notice that every billet is visited on the same night by a priest, Kappler will put two and two together—and make it *you*, Monsignor."

As a compromise it was agreed that the priests would not enter any billet unless they had made sure it was not under observation. Those of O'Flaherty's helpers who had Vatican passes allowing them to ignore the curfew worked through the bitter winter night, walking swiftly from home to home, ever watchful for the SS or Koch's neo-Fascist Gestapo. At some billets they found parties in progress, and because of the curfew such parties were always all-night affairs. The priests warned the escapers who were visiting another billet not to go back to their own premises the next morning without checking.

At dawn scores more priests went into action. Like Father Owen Sneddon ("Horace", the New Zealander), a number of these priests were saved from arrest only by the porters of the big apartment blocks. Father Sneddon had the most dangerous job of all—checking on the Via Firenze apartment. He approached it slowly, head bent down over his breviary, to be stopped by a sibilant hiss when he was a few yards from the main doors. The Italian porter was standing in the doorway, his face conveying an unmistakable message. Silently Father Sneddon walked on past, to be joined a little way up the street by the porter, who told him what had happened.

For days the whole organization worked frantically, moving men to new billets, changing the whole system so that any one person would know the whereabouts of perhaps only half-a-dozen men at a time, and generally doing everything possible to restore the situation after the disasters of the first days of January. It proved for a time impossible to learn the fate of the men now in Regina Coeli. Derry asked Sir D'Arcy Osborne in a formal memorandum if the Swiss could visit the prison and see what could be done for Furman and the others, but Sir D'Arcy and the Swiss diplomats said "no", and for a very good reason that had not occurred to the soldier Derry. This was that many of the prisoners in Regina Coeli were held under false names and it was probable that the Germans did not even know they were British. If, however, the Swiss went into the prison and visited these men, the Germans would at once want to know just how the Swiss were aware of their very existence in the prison. Kappler would, correctly, assume that the information came from the British Legation and O'Flaherty, which would hopelessly compromise the Vatican.

Molly Stanley did her best but, while she could move fairly freely in the Italian section of the prison, she was not allowed into the section controlled by the German SS and Koch's sadistic torturers, a section where night after night the cries of men being interrogated could be heard by the other prisoners in their cells. Somehow, however, Molly did make contact with Buchner and she brought a message that he wanted to see the Monsignor. Now while Derry kept O'Flaherty fully informed on every aspect of the organization, except its occasional espionage activities, and O'Flaherty dutifully informed Derry of everything he was doing that touched on prisoners-of-war, especially British, the Monsignor did not always disclose all his plans in advance. He knew quite well that Derry would have been aghast had he known at the time that O'Flaherty frequently slipped into Regina Coeli to see what he could do for the prisoners, and O'Flaherty certainly could guess what the major would say if he learned now of the message from Buchner which could, after all, very well be another trap.

Traps were the last thing to worry O'Flaherty if there was a human being in need. He went to the prison and saw Bruno in his cell. Bruno had been "questioned" by Koch, acknowledged master of tortures both crude and refined. (One of Koch's devices was a leather belt studded with long narrow steel spikes on the inside which could be gradually tightened round the naked waist of a man—or a woman.) In Bruno's case they had, over days, filed his teeth down one by one in an attempt to make him reveal what he knew about the escape organization. For one brief moment Furman saw Bruno being half-pushed, half-carried by two warders back to his cell after one interrogation session. Bruno managed to force a smile to his bruised and bloody face. Now in a cell two floors below ground-level, Bruno the Communist looked up from his bunk at the priest and said simply, "I only wanted to tell you, Monsignor, that I have not talked—and I won't." He never did. A few days later he was shot by the SS.

Now the Germans attacked O'Flaherty on three fronts. Kappler was convinced that the Monsignor was the moving spirit behind the whole organization and he had two conversations, one with Baron von Weiszacker and the other with Prince Bismarck, the German Minister to Italy. Neither of these men were in any way pro-Nazi. As the first result the long-suffering Rector of the Collegio Teutonicum in his turn had a conversation with O'Flaherty.

"There is nothing I can do about your own activities, Monsignor. However much I may sympathize with your priestly motives I cannot help you, and I will do my best not to hinder you", said the Rector. "But the … um … 'visitor' you have had in your room for some weeks now, I'm afraid he must go. This I can insist upon and I do. Will you please see to it in the course of the next few days?"

O'Flaherty knew when he was beaten and he went to Sir D'Arcy Osborne, the man walking the diplomatic tightrope these days. Sir D'Arcy said at once, "Well Hugh, the only thing is for Major Derry to move in with me. I know it will make things more complicated in some ways but in others it can possibly help. He must come into the Legation and once inside he must not leave it—for an instant."

Derry made the move that evening, being escorted past the Swiss Guards in O'Flaherty's clothes for the last time, and then settled down in the Hospice Santa Marta, a virtual prisoner, for what was to prove almost five months.

Within a day or two O'Flaherty was summoned to the Vatican Secretariat. The position, from a Vatican point of view, was getting out of hand. Apart from the representations made by von Weiszacker, O'Flaherty's definite unpopularity with some of the Italians in the Vatican Civil Service made matters worse for him. Foreigners of any nationality have never been welcomed in the Vatican service and O'Flaherty's unique rise to office in the Urban College, his career in the Diplomatic Service, and his appointment to the Holy Office had all been viewed with envious distaste by many Italians. Not even all of his fellow Irishmen approved of what he was doing. Twenty years after it all, one Irish priest who was in Rome at the time, was to write, "Some of us felt it was scarcely fair. What would Britain have said if the roles were reversed and the Germans were using the Vatican for such purposes?" Though exactly what transpired at the interview was kept secret, O'Flaherty was a subdued man—for a few hours. Years later he admitted, "I had my knuckles rapped pretty hard."

Still pondering on his inner struggle between determination to do what he could to help anyone in distress and his priestly obligation of obedience to the will of the Vatican, O'Flaherty, alone in his study now that Derry was in the British Legation, whistled with surprise when the porter brought him up a large envelope containing a gilt-edged invitation to a dinner party at the Hungarian Embassy. He could not help wondering if this was a more-than-usually subtle trap but did not dream of turning down the invitation. There were not many guests, but Prince Bismarck and Baron von Weiszacker were both there among them. It was not until near the end of the evening that von Weiszacker drew the Monsignor to one side of the ornate drawing room and said, "My dear Monsignor, you know my private views and attitudes very well. Nobody in Rome honors you more than I do for what you are doing. But it has gone too far for all of us. Kappler is waiting in the hall, feeling rather frustrated, I am afraid. I am aware that he has made several ... er, informal ... and highly-irregular attempts to capture you—which he should not have done. Now, I have told him that you will of course have safe conduct back to the Vatican tonight. But ... if you ever step outside Vatican territory again, on whatever pretext, you will be arrested at once. Despite the consequences one could foresee, that decision has been agreed in your case and I cannot alter it. Now will you please think about what I have said?"

O'Flaherty smiled down at von Weiszacker and in a cheerful voice that carried across the soft hum of conversation in the room, replied, "Your Excellency is too considerate. I will certainly think about what you have said ... sometimes!"

He was a little more cautious now on the much rarer occasions when he did go out but he did not let the German edict—or the instructions from the Vatican Secretariat, which probably also included a ban on leaving the Vatican territory, deter him in the slightest when a real necessity arose. True, he practically confined his journeys to night time, but, as he saw it, with Derry incarcerated in the British Legation, it was even more important to keep a close personal watch on things.

Though only small in numbers, some of O'Flaherty's most active helpers in Rome and certainly, after the Yugoslavians, the most anti-German, were the men of the Freedom or Death Greek underground movement. One of the leaders was Evangelo Averoff, who years later, as Foreign Minister of Greece, was to adopt a very different attitude to all things British at the time of the Cyprus dispute. Early in December he had visited O'Flaherty with his friend Theodore Meletiou. They were introduced to Derry and rather flabbergasted him by announcing that they had found an elite band of British escapers at Arezzo, 120 miles from Rome—no less than three generals, an air vice-marshal, and four brigadiers. Derry was certain that Rome was not the safest place for such a distinguished collection of "brass", but gave Meletiou ten thousand lire for the officers and suggested he try to lead one of them back to Rome. Derry then forgot all about the incident until, on January 13, O'Flaherty made his routine daily visit to him in the Hospice Santa

Marta. This day he was wearing his enormous infectious smile as he handed Derry a letter signed by Major General M. D. Gambier-Parry, who was in fact now the senior British escaper in all Italy. Meletiou had brought him and Mrs. Mary Boyd, an Englishwoman who had helped escapers in the Arezzo area, to Rome, and the general now wanted to know if he could get into the Vatican with or without the assistance of the British Minister. Under current circumstances smuggling the general into the Vatican was impossible, the Germans would immediately learn from their Vatican spies of an addition to the number of officially-interned officers, and Derry asked O'Flaherty if there was instead any specially safe billet where Gambier-Parry might be hidden.

"Ah now, me boy," boomed O'Flaherty, delighted to have the answer ready, "I've got just the place. I've been keeping it in reserve, ye might say, in case we had any distinguished visitors—or had to hide you! We'll get Brother Bob to take him there."

Brother Bob—"Whitebows"—who had already taken the general and Mrs. Boyd some money, now escorted the general to the home of Signora di Rienzo in Via Roggero Bonghi. The English-born Signora and her husband had had a secret room constructed in their house, which was shaped like an L, by walling up the door of a fourth-floor room at the end of one arm of the L. From inside the house there was no way of telling of the room's existence and it could only be entered through the window after crossing a plank, forty feet above the ground, from the window of a passage running down the other arm of the L. It was the perfect hiding place, the di Rienzos were wonderful hosts, and Gambier-Parry was relatively happy for a time. But as the weeks passed the forced inactivity made him fret, he wanted to be doing something. This was clear in the many letters he wrote to O'Flaherty and to Derry. O'Flaherty sent "Whitebows" to collect the general one evening without telling Derry who, he knew quite well, would have been outraged at the idea. They took a streetcar to the Vatican and there was a beaming O'Flaherty and a small crowd of his Irish and aristocratic friends waiting in the piazza.

As O'Flaherty, in full monsignorial robes, shepherded his group across the piazza to the right-hand entrance to the Vatican and the Papal apartments, he put a massive arm round the shoulders of the distinguished-looking, gray-haired general and practically roared out introductions as they passed the saluting Swiss Guards.

"This is an Irish doctor friend of mine", he said. "He's invited to His Holiness' reception also!" For some hours the general mixed with Roman society and the Diplomatic Corps—including von Weiszacker and Prince Bismarck—at the Pope's birthday reception. O'Flaherty blandly introduced Gambier-Parry to both German diplomats and the ever-cordial Bismarck promptly invited "the doctor" to visit him. "I will try", replied Gambier-Parry, finding it a hard job to avoid laughing at the mischievous expression on O'Flaherty's rubicund face and the look of quiet enjoyment on Sir D'Arcy Osborne's ivory visage.

Next morning Sam Derry did what he could to take the Monsignor to task! He pointed out the unwarranted risk involved in the exploit but was charmingly put off by O'Flaherty with the typical remark, "Now sure, the poor fellow needed a breath of air, he's been cooped up for weeks. We could all do with exercise, Patrick . . . 'tis a pity I haven't brought me clubs over, we could get in a bit of putting practice—nothing like golf for knocking the troubles of this poor world out of your mind!" But O'Flaherty did agree that if General Gambier-Parry was prepared to exchange a little security and some luxury for a bit more freedom, he could be moved, and he became a "patient" at the hospital of the Little Sisters of Mary (the "Blue Nuns") at San Stefano Rotondo, where he could exercise in the grounds, and he stayed there until the liberation of Rome.

By mid-January the flood of escapers into Rome reached peak proportions. There were numbers of Indians, including renegades and spies, and a steady flow of Arabs who would turn up at the Arco delle Campane to demand Christian sanctuary! O'Flaherty, of course, would help anyone, but at the firm insistence of Derry it was left to John May to handle these highly-suspect Arabs. They were never billetted in any way by the organization, but given a monthly sum of money and told to hide themselves in Rome or the nearby countryside, which they managed to do very well.

While coping with problems like this, O'Flaherty and Derry were shocked by another escape for their heroic Mrs. Chevalier.

CHAPTER ELEVEN

Spying for England!

AT THIS TIME Mrs. Chevalier had four British escapers (Flood, Martin, O'Neill and Stokes) and one South African named Matthews in the apartment. One January evening about ten minutes before curfew she answered a knock at the door. An Italian boy of about seventeen, lame in one leg and quite unknown to her, whispered urgently, "The Germans are going to raid you tonight. If your soldiers get ready now I will take them to my house until it it is safe—but you only have a few minutes!" Mrs. Chevalier felt she could believe the boy, but dare she take the chance? She told the five soldiers who, true to their pledge to Derry to do anything rather than compromise "Mummie", as they now called her, at once followed the boy into the night.

On the hour of curfew, almost to the second, the SS pounded on the door and the raid commander strode in to face Mrs. Chevalier, five girls and Paul, examined their papers, glanced around the apartment, almost casually, and then asked more or less politely, "Who else lives in this apartment, Signora?"

"Only the family, here," answered Mrs. Chevalier, "and there is barely room for them."

"That I can understand", said the SS man. "Nonetheless we have been told that men are seen coming and going all the time from this building and they include British prisoners-of-war whom you are hiding. What have you to say to that?"

"Simply . . . where could I possibly put them?" Mrs. Chevalier replied. Before the SS commander could ask any more questions a couple of troopers who had been going through the other rooms, came into the kitchen, each giving a quick shake of the head in response to the commander's unspoken query.

"Well, Signora, it does seem as if you have an enemy", said the commander. "Someone must have given false information. Have you any idea who might do such a thing?"

Mrs. Chevalier thought she had a very good idea indeed who had denounced her—the Fascist neighbors in the very next apartment. Gesturing to the wall she said, "You are right, there have been a lot of visitors to this building, but I think most of them have been going next door!"

For the next half hour or so the Chevaliers sat in their kitchen listening delightedly to the Germans thoroughly wrecking the Fascists' home. While the girls had a hard time to refrain from laughing out loud, Mrs. Chevalier sat silently, darning some of the escapers' socks.

Neither O'Flaherty nor Derry were amused. Danger had again come far too near gallant "Mrs. M". Derry ordered that none of the men should return to the apartment and, knowing Mrs. Chevalier's tenacity, he did not protest when O'Flaherty said that, German ban or not, he would go and talk to her himself. He explained the decision. She pleaded hard to have her "boys" back but O'Flaherty was adamant. The five soldiers were moved to the home of Cecarelli, the butcher, in one of the outer suburbs, and to soothe Mrs. Chevalier it was arranged that she would continue to be responsible for feeding them.

The next Gestapo raid was on the Lucidi apartment, to which Simpson had now returned to share a room with a Polish saboteur, complete with bag of gelignite! Everyone was in bed when the SS came thundering on the door, but in seconds the explosives were hidden, the Pole was unprotestingly thrust into bed with Peppina, the housemaid, while Simpson was told to pretend to be Renzo's half-witted nephew! Film director Lucidi had never directed a more bizarre plot. The Germans more or less ignored Simpson and the Pole but they arrested Renzo's eighteen-year-old stepson Gerard . . . and returned the following night to arrest Renzo himself, Simpson and the Pole meanwhile having fled to another billet.

It so happened that Gerard, Adrienne's son by her former marriage, was French, and Derry got De Vial at the French Embassy to persuade the Vichy French Ambassador to obtain the release of the youth and of Renzo.

The same night as the raid on the Lucidi's apartment, which apparently had nothing to do with the organization, O'Flaherty got news of the arrest of Concetta Piazza, code-named "Midwife", who was district nurse in a country district a few miles north of Rome. She had twenty British escapers hidden in her area, and it was she who kept them supplied with money and food. Fortunately, when she was arrested she had already distributed everything for that week. She guessed she had been denounced, which meant that the Germans probably had little real evidence against her, and when she was taken to Regina Coeli she wrote, on prison toilet paper, a long letter to Field Marshal von Kesselring, protesting that a nurse such as herself, who had helped everyone including Germans, was being prevented from doing her vital and hygienic work out of mere suspicion. The letter was first brought to O'Flaherty, who discussed it with Derry. Obviously the letter would have to be properly typed on decent paper, fit for the eyes of a German hygienically-minded field marshal, but then how was it to be delivered to him?

At that moment Blon Kiernan dropped in for one of her frequent visits to the Monsignor and, being told the problem, said gaily, "Daddy can do it!" She took the letter back to the Irish Legation and it was duly forwarded to the German commander in chief, marked in Dr. Kiernan's own hand, "For the personal attention of Field Marshal von Kesselring." "Midwife" was released a day or two later, without a word of explanation.

Events were now moving fast. The Allied Fifth Army had opened its main offensive on January 12 with advances by the French, British and American Corps, and at two A.M. on January 22 the VI Corps landed on the Anzio beaches, the First British Division to the north of the town and the Third United States Division to the south. Progress was swift at first but then the Germans dug in, and with reinforcements rushed from France, Yugoslavia and the Reich itself, counter-attacked. For the Allies also reinforcement and an uninterrupted flow of supplies to the beachhead were all-essential, and O'Flaherty must have been as fully aware of this as anyone else when one day at the beginning of February and wearing such a very innocent smile on his face, he said to Derry, "My boy, there is a lot of funny business going on. The mouth of the Tiber is crammed with wee motorboats. Now Patrick, what d'ye think they'd be for?" One of his small army of priests had sent in this report. Derry reacted instantly and sent one of the officer escapers to reconnoitre. When the officer came back and reported what was going on, Derry could hardly wait to get the news back to British Intelligence via one of his

mobile radio transmitters operated by a park-bench Romeo.
The "wee motorboats" were German E-boats, brought all
the way overland across Italy from the Adriatic in a bid to
cut the Allied supply lines to the Anzio beachhead. After
the liberation of Rome, General Alexander, Allied commander in chief in Italy and later field marshal, told
O'Flaherty and Derry that the information had been invaluable as the Allies had had no idea that the Germans at this
time had any E-boats on the west coast of Italy. The boats
they did get over so laboriously were promptly blown to
pieces by the R.A.F. and the Anzio buildup continued.

Understandably it was when activities of this positively
non-neutral nature became known to, or at least suspected
by, the Vatican authorities that O'Flaherty, despite the indul-
gent attitude of Cardinal Ottaviani, was in deep disgrace.
It is as well that none of his superiors could ever have
learned of his next adventure into the field of anti-Nazi
espionage, for this deeply involved Delia and Blon Kiernan at the Irish Legation, who probably were quite unconscious of the fact that through the Monsignor they were
being used by Derry's intelligence service in the Allied cause.
Prince Bismarck, who was second-in-command at the German Embassy to Italy, was a close friend of O'Flaherty
and of the Kiernans, and so, when Derry wanted some
vital information out of the Germans' own mouths, so to
speak, the way in which he might get it was obvious. The
key question was whether the Germans would in the last
resort defend Rome or declare it an open city. If they
intended to fight for the capital the escape organization
would be wrecked; if they intended to retreat northward
it was Derry's military duty to preserve the organization as
completely as possible and enable every possible escaper to
link up with his own unit once more. The information,

one way or the other, would also be of tremendous impor-
tance to General Alexander.

O'Flaherty contrived an invitation for Blon to have tea
at the German Embassy, and on her return to O'Flaherty at
the Collegio Teutonicum she reported that Prince Bismarck
was quite convinced that the Wehrmacht would have to
withdraw, not fight for Rome. O'Flaherty at once told Derry,
who radioed the information south to Allied Intelligence.
Derry also issued an order through Simpson that all the
escapers were to be kept undercover as far as possible until
the liberation of the city, which nearly everyone now
expected was only a matter of a week or two. Derry's fear
was that the men would act carelessly and precipitately in
the excitement of the time and get themselves arrested and
shot outright rather than sent to a prison camp. But the
next two or three days suggested that most people had been
too optimistic about the Allied advance and Prince Bismarck
too pessimistic about the German resistance. Far from preparing to pull out, the Germans were packing Rome with
troops from the north and Derry's radio operators were kept
busy reporting these movements—and more tea-table chatter from Blon about top-level German reactions. In the longer term her reports proved very accurate.

On January 24 Rino Messina, an Italian barber who went
most days into Regina Coeli to shave the prisoners as part
of the German hygiene regulations, brought Derry via May
a tiny slip of paper on which Furman had been able to
make a remarkably comprehensive report, including a list
of the escapers he knew to be in the prison. None had
been interrogated so far. This was encouraging news, but
two days later came another letter from Furman, reporting
that all British prisoners were being taken out of the jail for
an unknown destination. On February 14, O'Flaherty was

working at his desk in the Holy Office when a priest slipped into the room and said meaningly, "Hugh, there are a couple of your 'friends' in the piazza!" O'Flaherty, who never knew what to expect on such occasions, hurried to the Arco delle Campane and out into the vast square. As he saw who was standing there, his eyes lit up and he let out a great roar, utterly heedless of everyone, including the Nazi paratroop guards on the perimeter.

"In the name of God, it's good to see you, John!" he bellowed and hugged Furman to him. With Furman was Lieutenant J. E. Johnstone, R.E., one of the officers who had been at Chieti. Furman and Johnstone had jumped from the train taking them at thirty miles per hour through northern Italy when it was only a few miles from the Swiss border, and with the help of various Italians they hitchhiked and cycled their way to Rome. It was the third escape for each man. Bubbling with pleasure, O'Flaherty took them now to St. Monica's Monastery near the Holy Office and left them with Fathers Claffey and Tracey while he went back to tell Derry. He returned with one of his own suits for Johnstone (nobody knew how many suits the Monsignor had, but he never seemed to run out of them) and in a few moments there was an excited and happy reunion with Simpson and Renzo Lucidi under the noses of the Germans in the middle of St. Peter's Square. Derry, of course, could not go out of the Hospice Santa Marta.

Furman went right back to work with Simpson. Conditions were more difficult than ever. The rationing system had broken down completely and Romans were still waiting for their November, December and January entitlements. The water supply was completely cut off on some days; on others it was available only for an hour or two; there were frequent electricity failures and it could take two hours to boil a kettle of water on a gas stove. The Germans now encouraged the Italians to bring food in from the countryside and this eased the shortage to some extent, but prices went sky high and Simpson and Furman had to persuade Derry to raise the allowance to the *padrones* so that the escapers could be fed. This took some doing because Derry and Sir D'Arcy Osborne were seriously perturbed about finance.

Raids were continuous, again not on account of the escape organization but now by the Germans to get forced labor for Rome's defence works and by the Fascist Gestapo against black-marketeers, with whom the organization was so deeply involved. It was felt unwise that Simpson and Furman should share the same billet, and Furman went to live with an Italian clerk, Romeo Giuliani, and his family, which included an eighteen-year-old son, Gino. It was Furman who brought the Chevalier apartment back into operation, as an emergency. He had learned that an Italian, who had guided four escapers into Rome and had been arrested, was in the Via Tasso SS headquarters, where he probably would talk sooner or later. The Italian knew no details about the organization but he did know where he had guided the escapers, so Furman promptly shifted them to Mrs. Chevalier's and only just in time, for their original billet was raided a few hours after they had gone.

Mrs. Chevalier came spectacularly to the rescue again in a few days. One way or another the organization was able to provide simple medical care for the escapers and had been coping well with the minor illnesses arising from the hard winter and sometimes scant rations, but now a serious emergency arose. O'Flaherty went to Derry's room in the Legation and said, "We have a man with acute appendicitis and peritonitis on our hands. He's a Scotsman and he is at Subiaco, some miles from Rome."

"Well," said Derry, "we can't set up an operating theater there. He's got to get into a hospital. The best thing is to have him brought into Rome and left outside the German Embassy. Blon could perhaps see to it that Bismarck or someone is tipped off and they'll get him into the hospital. He'll lose his freedom of course, but it can't be helped."

"Whitebows" was sent to tell Private Norman Anderson of the Cameron Highlanders of the plan, but he came back to say that Anderson had flatly refused! "He says he'd rather die than give himself up, or be given up, to the Germans", reported Brother Bob. Derry looked despairingly at O'Flaherty. "I don't know what we can do, Monsignor. We can't let him die and it seems we can't save him either."

"Give me a couple of hours, me boy, and I may be able to fix up something", said O'Flaherty thoughtfully. "I've a wee plan that just might work."

Back in his own office O'Flaherty first telephoned his old friend Professor Albano, a distinguished surgeon at the Regina Elona Lazzaretto, a big hospital crammed now with German wounded from the Anzio battle. Next he sent for Father "Spike" Buckley, a man almost as big as himself, and finally he telephoned Delia Kiernan at the Irish Legation.

What Mrs. Kiernan would have done if her husband had called for his car with its diplomatic "CD" plates is problematical, but there were three reasons for the top-speed dash through the night that Father Buckley now undertook. One was Anderson's condition, the other was the possibility that the Irish Minister would miss his car, and the third was the fact that there was to be some sort of inspection of the Regina Elona Lazzaretto that very night and Professor Albano had told O'Flaherty that while he would certainly operate on a "friend" and forget the whole incident, the man must be removed from the hospital the minute the operation was over; he could not even be left in a ward long enough to recover from the anaesthetic.

When the Irish Legation car arrived outside the hospital, driven by Father Buckley, Brother Bob was cradling Anderson in his arms in the back of the car. Father Buckley took the soldier in his arms like a boy, carried him up the steps and across to the elevator. On the operating theater floor he was met by an Italian nursing sister who pointed to a stretcher-trolley standing empty outside the theater doors. Father Buckley laid Anderson on the stretcher and covered his body with a blanket, then stood waiting, holding the soldier's hand, until the theater doors opened and a stretcher was wheeled out. The sister at once pushed Anderson's stretcher in and Father Buckley walked down to the far end of the corridor to wait and pray. It was almost an hour before the theater doors opened again and the same sister pushed the trolley down the corridor to the elevator. Wordlessly she folded back the blanket and waited while Father Buckley lifted the unconscious Anderson in his arms once more, stepped into the elevator and so down to the main hall where Brother Bob had also been waiting and praying.

"Where to?" asked Father Buckley as he let in the clutch of the car, looking back over his shoulder at "Whitebows" who was holding Anderson sitting upright against him.

"'Mrs. M's', she will look after him better than anyone and besides Milko's there to see to the dressings", said Brother Bob, and in ten minutes Anderson was on a mattress laid on the table in the dining room of Mrs. Chevalier's apartment. Father Borg had already warned her of the emergency and Milko Scofic was waiting to take over. While they were discussing the situation Furman arrived in some agitation. He had heard that the apartment might be under observation (as in fact it was) and came to warn Mrs. Chevalier to make sure that anyone who might be there could get away in a hurry. That was one thing Anderson could not do, indeed he was only just now coming round from his anaesthetic.

"We'd better take him somewhere else", said Furman sensibly enough and Father Buckley agreed, adding, "If he does not get rest now he'll be a corpse before morning."

Here the gentle Mrs. Chevalier put her foot down. Despite her respect for priests, she practically stormed at the small group of men. "He stays here, and he will be quite safe!"

Anderson stayed but even Mrs. Chevalier now began to show signs of the strain of the following week. Five escapers who had been forced to flee other billets had been sharing the dining room, but now they slept in the box-room and the corridor, the girls were forbidden to play their gramophone, and the only people permitted to enter the sickroom were Mrs. Chevalier and Milko. Professor Albano had made a quick telephone call to O'Flaherty to say that his "friend" had survived the operation but was in a grave condition, and for several days Anderson hovered between life and death while Mrs. Chevalier and her hushed and nervous girls kept ceaseless watch for any signs of another raid.

On the seventh evening, again shortly before curfew, the lame Italian boy turned up once more. Now he simply told Mrs. Chevalier, "You are to be raided in two hours."

This was better notice than usual and just as well. First Mrs. Chevalier told her five escapers to get away and then sent Rosie to O'Flaherty since it would have been madness to use the telephone. O'Flaherty had one hour to do something.

"Delia," his voice came urgently over the telephone to Mrs. Kiernan, "get the car—somehow—and pick up Father Buckley. Our sick friend must be moved in a hurry."

Delia Kiernan sent off the Legation car. Anderson was still in a fair amount of pain when Father Buckley gathered him up in his arms yet again and carried him down the flights of stairs to the street. Mrs. Chevalier was in tears, certain that Anderson could not survive this journey. But he did. He was taken to the safest hideout of all, the American College, and given into the care of Colin Lesslie, who nursed him back to complete health in about a month.

Shortly after this O'Flaherty called on the services of another medical man willing to risk his life to save another. He had asked Milko Scofic to come and see him without delay.

"We have an American Air Force man in the Via Aurelia Antica billet, Milko", said O'Flaherty. "He had a head injury when he bailed out of his aircraft but didn't seem too bad at first. Now it is clear that he will have to have an operation, probably to relieve pressure on the brain. Professor Albano is away from Rome for a few days and in any event I can't get hold of a certain car I've used in the past, for I've tried and the owner is using it. Have you any ideas— and quickly, for this man is in a desperate condition."

"If it is a matter of the brain, Monsignor, who better than my own Professor of Neural Surgery at the University? Do you know Urbani?" replied Milko.

O'Flaherty sighed in relief. "Of course. I will telephone him while you go over there and if he agrees you can arrange the details with him."

Urbani said he would be delighted to help and between the Professor and Milko a proper ambulance was organized this time. When the ambulance drew up outside the San

Giovanni Hospital, Professor Urbani was standing waiting for it. He signalled to two military medical orderlies in the hall behind him and, as they slid out of the ambulance the stretcher on which the American lay, covered up to his eyes, Urbani explained, "A very high Party member indeed. Air-raid case. Get him to the theater at once."

The operation, in which Milko assisted the Professor, lasted nearly two hours, but it was successful and the American was taken back in the ambulance to Via Aurelia Antica, where Milko visited him daily until he was fully recovered. (Milko married an art student who used to go around Rome's restaurants and cafes, drawing portraits and caricatures of Allied escapers. Her name? Gina Lollobrigida.)

Another time O'Flaherty organized an appendicitis operation entirely on his own. His own original starting point in Rome, the Propaganda College, held a number of men evading arrest (not Allied escapers). They lived in outbuildings in the grounds, as at the American College. One of them, an Austrian, came down with appendicitis. Borrowing a car, this time from a high Vatican official, O'Flaherty drove himself to the Propaganda College, collected the Austrian and took him to the Santo Spirito Hospital. Here the nuns put the wanted man into a ward almost full of German officers, prepared him for the operation, and slipped him onto the theater list of a German military surgeon, who whipped out the appendix without the faintest idea of the identity of his patient. The Austrian was even given a few days to recover partly in the ward before O'Flaherty arrived to take him back to the Propaganda College.

CHAPTER TWELVE

"Hot Line" to SS Headquarters

WHILE THE Vatican City escaped harm in the air raids, the small town that grew up around the Pope's summer residence, Castel Gandolfo, near Albano, was heavily hit by American aircraft on February 10 and something like five hundred refugees were killed. What the furious Italian public did not know was that the Germans had set up a whole complex of repair workshops in the main square of the town, one high-walled side of which forms a boundary to the Papal estate. The Vatican authorities appreciated the reason for the attack, however inefficiently it was mounted, and they had another problem at Castel Gandolfo that fell to O'Flaherty to solve for them. Paul Freyberg, a young lieutenant in the Grenadier Guards, and son of General Bernard Freyberg, V.C., commander of the New Zealand Corps, had been captured near Anzio but escaped and reached Castel Gandolfo. Seeing the proclamation on the wall of the Papal estate that this was extra-territorial property, he claimed sanctuary and, to the embarrassment of the Vatican authorities back in Rome, was admitted. This was the one occasion when the Secretariat decided to make covert use of their "problem Monsignor" for whom they knew this would be more or less routine work!

O'Flaherty discussed the Freyberg situation with Derry, who agreed that the young officer would be a terrific prestige prize for the Germans if he were recaptured but pointed out that to get him into the Vatican he would have to be brought along the main road from the battlefront.

"This time it is easy", said O'Flaherty cheerfully. "You see the Vatican powers-that-be have had a fleeting change of heart about sanctuary, especially for a general's son, and they will shut their eyes to my little plan."

Freyberg was taken the eighteen miles to Rome crushed into the trunk of the official Vatican car that visited Castel Gandolfo weekly with supplies. Within a day or two of his arrival, Derry learned that Freyberg was about to have his twenty-first birthday and this obviously called for a party, the only "official" one that the organization ever gave until the liberation of Rome. The party was held in Derry's room at the Legation, May working wonders with his black market friends, and even Furman—who had not met Derry since his return to the capital—was smuggled in by Princess Nini Pallavicini. On one of Furman's visits to the Collegio Teutonicum the Princess explained that the day chosen for the party had been so selected because it was a Church feast day and it was customary on such days for a number of people to attend Mass in the chapel on the ground floor of the Hospice Santa Marta and then join one or other of the small parties given by the diplomats on the floors above.

"You just stay in the center of my group. There will be eight of us," she said, "and I don't think there will be any trouble."

When the time came, the Princess led her flock at a leisurely pace across the courtyard from the Collegio Teutonicum to the Hospice. Furman, trying to look inconspicuous in the middle, could not help smiling at the smart salutes from the gendarmerie. On the third floor he found Derry, Freyberg, some of the other interned British officers and, as the day wore on, many of O'Flaherty's other helpers. Sir D'Arcy Osborne and the Legation Secretary, Hugh Montgomery, joined in also, and quietly in one corner Sir D'Arcy, who had asked no questions as to how Furman had possibly gained entry, reassured the young officer of the value of the work that was being done.

Apart from the work of rescue, more and more military information was being gathered by the organization and passed on. On one trip the Liberty or Death leaders Averoff and Meletiou took three hundred pounds, a load of clothing and dozens of pairs of boots stolen from the German depot right up into northern Italy for the Greek escapers concentrated there. They also took a camera which, if it had been found, would have earned them a firing squad at once. Back in three weeks, Averoff not only brought lists of escapers and the names and addresses of their next-of-kin, but notes on the disposition of German forces in the north and a whole series of photographs of the Nazi preparations for a last-ditch defence on the Italian side of the French border.

Ever since the shattering series of SS raids in January the apartments at Via Firenze and Via Domenico Cellini had been abandoned by the organization. The Cellini apartment indeed was now occupied by Ubaldo Cipolla in whose name it was registered when he first obtained it for O'Flaherty. And Cipolla was now known to the organization as a double agent!

Thus it was with a terrific shock one morning at the beginning of March that Renzo Lucidi answered his telephone and heard a voice from the dead—that of Joe Pollak. For Joe was in the Cipollas' apartment. However, Cipolla was backing any horse in the field, as Derry knew, and was to play an important and helpful role yet in rescue

operations. Renzo hurried to Via Domenico Cellini with a
new suit of clothes for Joe and took him to Simpson's billet. Joe was in an appalling condition as a result of the hard-
ships he had suffered, and, though it was not known for
some time, he already had tuberculosis.

When Joe was taken back to Sulmona with Iride they
found all the main helpers in the organization in that area
and many of the escapers had been arrested, as "Dick",
the Australian medical orderly, had denounced everyone
he knew. All were taken to Aquila to stand trial on different charges. Joe was charged as a traitor and a spy because
the Germans soon discovered he was of Czech origin and
thus a citizen of the Greater Reich. He was beaten up
again and again and kept in a cell without any form of
heating, with no blankets, developing pneumonia which
led to the tuberculosis. When everyone was assembled for
the trial, waiting for a few minutes in a courtyard, Joe
managed to get "Dick" to one side and told him that if
he would retract his denunciations and say he made them
when he was drunk, he, Joe, would do his best to see that
the Allies did not execute "Dick" for his treachery. The
traitor looked thoughtful and Joe knew exactly what he
was thinking. Whatever happened to anyone else, Pollak
was certain to die for the Germans had refused to recog-
nize him as a prisoner-of-war, and a dead Pollak could
not do anything to or for "Dick".

Then the amazing thing happened. When the men and
women about to stand trial were going to be marched into
the courtroom, there was a short delay to permit the admission to the jail of a new batch of prisoners. As these men
trudged wearily through the gates and past him, Joe recognized a British officer who had been at Chieti camp. Without much thought of the possible consequences, for it seemed

a miracle was happening, Joe broke ranks and limped across to the German guard commander.

"That officer can prove who I am", he gasped hoarsely.

The guard commander stared coldly at the tiny, frail, battered Cypriot-Czech. Something, nobody will ever know what exactly, made him pause and look harder.

"Halt", he barked, and the small column of POWs ground to a stop. The German commander stood by as Joe confronted the British officer and established his identity. Watching from the far side of the courtyard, "Dick" had to start thinking again—and came up with the right answer. Both Joe and "Dick" were sentenced merely to be returned to a POW camp, three of the others were sentenced to death and the others to imprisonment, but the three facing execution managed to escape.

Joe Pollak escaped from Aquila railway station during an RAF raid, while he was waiting to be entrained for Germany, and reached Rome after a trip that included some miles clinging to the underside of a truck on which he had got a lift, which was stopped by the Germans and driven to a barracks on the outskirts of the city . . . Joe dropping off neatly at the barracks gates. Truly Joe Pollak had a charmed life.

Cipolla's mind worked fast and when he and his Russian-born wife saw Joe Pollak, of all people, at the door of their apartment, it was the answer to whatever prayers they knew. Here was a chance of showing Monsignor O'Flaherty and his British helpers that Cipolla really was on the side of the Allies, even if he had helped the Germans and Fascists just a little from time to time. Cipolla did everything possible for Joe until Renzo arrived to take him away, and was quick to send a message to John May pointing out that he was on the side of the angels! This double-dealing suited Derry and even the now much more sophisticated O'Flaherty, and they played along with Cipolla, calculating that they never knew when he would be useful. As indeed he was to be, fairly soon at that.

At the beginning of March the organization had the sharp reminder that Kappler really meant business so far as O'Flaherty personally was concerned, when he tried to take the Monsignor from the rear, but they also had an equally acute and compensatory boost to morale over the extraordinary piece of subversion business fixed by May. To some extent the key men of the O'Flaherty organization worked independently, not surprisingly, considering their different characters: the unworldly Monsignor who was learning fast, the trained officer, Sam Derry, the arch-scrounger and super fiddler, John May. For some time May had been intrigued by the young Italian boy who had twice so accurately warned Mrs. Chevalier of danger and reputedly had access to the Gestapo orders-of-the-day. In his own way, he began checking up, finding out his friends and associates, getting them in his debt or making willing allies of them. At last he went to Derry one day wearing a grin instead of his usual discreet smile.

"How'd you like to read the daily routine orders from Via Tasso (SS headquarters)—in advance?" he asked without preamble.

The normally unflappable Derry gaped at him. May was not given to joking and surely this could be nothing else.

"That sounds too good to be true, John", he said. "But I'm too busy for fun today. What did you really come about?"

"Listen to me, sir", insisted May. "There's a character by the name of Giuseppe who says he had a pal in the Questora, a young clerk who can pinch copies of the daily orders as they're duplicated. You can make a very good guess who that might be—do you remember the young lad who twice tipped off 'Mrs. M' about raids?"

Derry did, and the fact that both tips proved correct.

"How much does Giuseppe want? I'm quite sure he won't do it for love."

"Only a thousand lire for the pair of them," said May, "and the Monsignor will have his own little way of getting the reports into the Vatican for us so that the communication line can't possibly be traced. It's worth a try, sir."

It was not only worth a try, it proved enormously successful on a limited plane. The very first report not only included the routine orders for the SS and neo-Fascist Gestapo troops searching for Communists and escapers, it even listed some of the districts of Rome where the Germans planned surprise raids during the next two or three nights. Teutonic insistence on committing everything to paper more than once proved the Nazis' undoing during the war. It was at once clear to Derry that Giuseppe would not be foolish enough to try to bluff them by sending information whose truth or otherwise would be exposed in a day or two. He had to be genuine. He was. Such billets as the organization had in the danger areas were temporarily evacuated and May and Derry sat back to wait. Right enough, the areas were raided, without success, and a day or two later the escapers moved back again into their homes. There was one flaw in the system that nothing could overcome and this was that the routine orders and even the list of "blitz raid" areas did not cover any swoops the German and Fascists might make if their suspicions were suddenly aroused in any district. These raids could happen at any time, at any place. Still, this was a risk to which everyone was accustomed. As copies of the daily orders continued to come in, O'Flaherty and Derry had a fresh and difficult problem. Curfew was now at 5.30 P.M. Public transport had more or less broken down and what did exist was under nonstop surveillance. Only O'Flaherty, Derry, Simpson and Byrnes knew the location of all billets. Derry and Byrnes were confined to the Vatican, O'Flaherty risked instant arrest if spotted anywhere a few yards or so from St. Peter's Square. Furman did not know many of the new billets that had been established while he was away. This meant that all the work fell on Simpson and O'Flaherty's team of priests, who were kept constantly travelling about the city, switching escapers from billet to billet, sometimes with only an hour or two to spare. Every second they were out and about these men risked ghastly torture and almost certain execution.

Giuseppe's reports became more and more precise and therefore more valuable. Often he was able to indicate that a particular raid was the result of a denouncement and Derry became seriously worried. The details given in the denouncements to the SS and Fascist Gestapo were almost always diabolically accurate. Plainly it was not the case, as Derry had thought at first, merely of Italians trying to ensure German goodwill because they now doubted if the Allies would ever arrive in Rome. Someone who really did *know* the organization was betraying it systematically and extremely cleverly, and would have been catastrophically successful but for Giuseppe who rushed the informer's reports to O'Flaherty as soon as they reached the Questura. A typical such report read "... a baker in the San Giovanni district is reported hiding some British and Badoglio soldiers in a walled-up garrett." He was, but not for long. The soldiers had fled when the Gestapo arrived and the baker was most convincingly indignant.

An even more ominous report from Giuseppe next confirmed Derry's half-formed feeling that the Germans were now dressing up agents as priests and sending them out into Rome to contact escapers and offer to take them to secure hiding places—as secure as the Regina Coeli prison. There came the day when Derry had to go to O'Flaherty and say, "Giuseppe's latest report is very disturbing, Monsignor. All approaches to the church of San Roberto Bellarmino are being watched. The Germans are certain the priests are hiding some escapers and providing money for others—as, of course, they are. Will you warn the priests to be especially careful? It is vital that the Germans get on to nothing that may lead irrefutably to you."

Normally O'Flaherty would have laughed off the warning, saying with deep conviction, "God will look after us all, me boy", but now things were different. When he himself had been able to move reasonably freely in Rome, even though taking considerable risks in the process, he had no hesitation in asking his priests to accept the same dangers. But as far as possible he flatly refused to let other men take risks he could not share, and he now agreed to do what Derry asked and the warning was duly passed on. Not in time. In a day or two the Free Frenchman de Vial made his way from the French Embassy to Derry and reported that Pasqualino Perfetti, the bogus priest who had guided Derry into Rome (and whom the major had disliked from the first) was the betrayer!

Perfetti had been in the organization from its very earliest days and knew the whereabouts of a large number of the British billets and probably all the French ones, for the French side had been his special responsibility. Apparently he had been arrested, handed over to Koch at his torture center in a block of flats on the Via Principe Amedeo, thoroughly beaten up, and then taken around Rome, bandaged and limping, by the Fascist Gestapo to point out one billet after the other. Giuseppe's next reports from the Questura confirmed this and showed that Perfetti had certainly gone the whole hog as an informer, not only guiding the Fascists to hideouts but in each case operating the secret signal to gain admission. He also gave Koch a list of everyone that he knew was in hiding. With such information Kappler and Koch could move swiftly and effectively, "routine orders" meant little, and within a few days twenty-one escapers had been recaptured and more than a dozen of the Italian *padrones* arrested.

CHAPTER THIRTEEN

A Fateful March

MARCH BROUGHT a succession of reverses for the organization. By the middle of the month O'Flaherty and Derry had 3,423 on the books and on any given night there were about 180 soldiers, sailors and airmen hidden in Rome. The organization had perfected many of its techniques and had been working fairly smoothly until it received a major psychological blow. This was the saturation bombing on February 15 of the great fifteen-hundred-year-old monastery of Monte Cassino, which stood on a height that formed the pivot of the whole, so far unbreakable, German defence line. The bombing has been the subject of strong controversy ever since. General Freyberg demanded a massive air attack before launching his infantry assault, and General Alexander agreed and accepted responsibility for it. There were no German troops in the monastery but their fortifications were, as Churchill put it, "hardly separate from the building itself". In the attack over 450 tons of bombs were dropped on this one objective—after the monks had been warned—and most of the monastery was destroyed. Wryly Churchill recorded, "The result was not good." Subsequent Allied infantry attacks failed repeatedly. The German line stood.

The result was not good in other terms either. The Catholic Italians, even the most consistently pro-Allied of them,

were utterly outraged. Nothing could make them see any
military necessity for the attack, particularly since it had
proved abortive, and O'Flaherty himself was appalled and
furious. His partly-subdued anti-British feelings boiled to
the surface once more, and his attitude was shared by nearly
all of his priestly helpers and his Irish associates. It fell to
Simpson and Furman to talk the *padrones* and the priests
back into a cooperative mood, but the atmosphere remained
tense and uncomfortable and might have gotten even worse
but for a German blunder that could only be compared
with Cassino in the magnitude of its effect on Italian morale.
This was the dreadful Ardeatine Massacre.

Before this, however, O'Flaherty had yet another narrow
escape—on the ever-fateful Ides of March, the fifteenth,
when Kappler made yet another attempt to catch him. On
the very next day "Whiteboys" (Brother Robert Pace) was
caught.

Among the variegated helpers of the organization was a
man named Grossi, one of O'Flaherty's earliest recruits. Kappler had captured him and a combination of mild torture
and the promise of cash induced Grossi to agree to betray
O'Flaherty. This was a rather better-planned plot than the
Germans' usual effort. Grossi was actually providing a billet
for two escapers and though he knew this, Kappler left them
strictly alone. Grossi went to see O'Flaherty at the Holy
Office, chatted about his escapers and then said, "They tell
me there are half a dozen more hiding near Fara Sabina
[about thirty miles from Rome] but I myself can't get them
into the city. One of the men is sick but I could soon get
him well again, I have plenty of pasta and vino!" Derry was
not present at this meeting and O'Flaherty had no intention of telling him about it. Totally incapable of resisting an
appeal on behalf of any person in trouble, O'Flaherty told

Grossi, "Well, I will have to be rather careful. The Germans are very keen on entertaining me, you know. But I think I can arrange to go out there to say Mass next Sunday, the Feast of Saint Joseph, and we can bring in the sick man at least and the others later, God willing."

It was a simple, straightforward plan ... if one allowed for the fact that the Gestapo might not be so vigilant on a Sunday morning and not keeping a watch on the church at Fara Sabina. Luck, and Giuseppe, was on the side of the Irish. On Saint Patrick's day, March 17, a telephone call interrupted the usual little party in O'Flaherty's room in the Collegio Teutonicum. Smilingly waving Father Buckley into silence and cutting short a heartrending performance of "Aghadoe", O'Flaherty picked up the telephone and listened. As he did so the smile left his ruddy face and his guests tensed uncomfortably.

"All right, I understand. God forgive him", said O'Flaherty, and put down the receiver. Never knowing what to expect, what disaster, what new threat the telephone would report, the guests stayed silent and looked at their host. May moved over to him. "Everything all right, Monsignor?" he asked gently.

"Oh yes, John", said O'Flaherty. "Yes, indeed. Our little friend was just after telling me not to go to Fara Sabina on Sunday. Apparently the Germans know all about our plan. Grossi ... Grossi is working with them. You had better tell Major Derry. There will be things he has to do."

There were indeed. Derry's foremost worry was that Grossi might know of Mrs. Chevalier's activities since her apartment was still back in service as the flow of escapers into the city continued undiminished. Derry at once wrote a note to Simpson who was responsible for this area, saying, "'Mrs. M' is a wonderful woman—but no idea of security.

It is essential that Grossi does not know that *we* know of his activities. . . ." To Derry's relief, Simpson was able to reply "'Mrs. M' etc., are fully aware of this gentleman's activities and are on guard."

Grossi, probably, was responsible for the capture of Brother Bob, for the trap into which "Whitebows" fell was almost identical with that laid for O'Flaherty. Up to now one of the most active and mobile of all O'Flaherty's assistants, Brother Bob received a more or less routine message, seemingly through the organization, that two escapers were to be collected from the outskirts of Rome and taken to a city billet. Brother Bob, as ever, collected his escapers with his usual efficiency and escorted them into Rome and on to the home of two Italians.

"Your *padrones*, Andrea Casadi and Vittorio Fantini", said Brother Bob once they were safely inside the billet. But the "escapers" pulled out pistols. The two Gestapo agents marched Brother Bob and the Italians at gunpoint through the streets of Rome to the notorious Via Principe Amedeo, and the merciless hands of Ludwig Koch. A week later Casadi and Fantini were shot and Brother Bob knew that all that could lie ahead for him was the ultimate in torture unless and until he betrayed everything he knew of the organization. He kept his head. He insisted that he had merely guided two people he had never met before to an address in Rome at the request of a village priest, and he added that if the Fascist Gestapo cared to check, they would find that he was well known to high-ranking German officers. A bit baffled, but thoroughly respectful of the SS, the Fascists permitted him to send a message to his Superior at the Mother House of the De la Salle Order, which was now being used as a hospital and casualty clearing station. While working at the hospital Brother Bob had looked after wounded Germans with as much devotion as he was displaying in his rescue work for Allied POWs, bringing them little presents and generally endearing himself to the tough Wehrmacht men. The German officers at the hospital looked on him as more or less a saint and an imperative message went back to Koch that Brother Bob was needed at the hospital—right away. The Fascists freed him, with distinct reluctance, but added the ominous warning that probably they would want him back for "further questions". Brother Bob's Superior and O'Flaherty had a quick telephone conversation once "Whitebows" was safely back at the hospital, and it was decided that he should "vanish". No member of the organization saw him again until the liberation of the city.

The very day that Brother Bob was released saw the start of the tragic Ardeatine affair. Just as they always committed every plan to paper, the Germans liked to carry out all routine operations in exactly the same manner, at the same time, unimaginatively, unvaryingly. This was an immense help to the militant underground when it came to laying ambushes, and the Communists had made a note of the fact that precisely at two o'clock every afternoon a considerable squad of German soldiers marched down the narrow Via Rasella in central Rome on their way to a bathhouse. On Wednesday, March 22, the column of soldiers entered the street and started down it. At two o'clock to the second they were marching past a garbage cart standing odorously alone to one side of the road. The cart was one gigantic time bomb and it went off with German precision. The street was a scene of carnage from one end to the other. Portions of bodies littered the road, every man in the column was a casualty and thirty-two were killed instantly or died of their wounds.

Derry, who mistrusted the impromptu sabotage operations that were mounted both by the formal forces of the Allies and their zealous and highly informal supporters, took action as soon as he heard of the explosion. He was sure the Germans would demand their usual eye-for-an-eye. Every possible billet was emptied at once and the escapers told to go and "hide" in parks or stand around the streets in crowds, do anything to keep inconspicuous, but above all make certain they did not involve the Italian *padrones*, for whom death was certain if caught, like Casadi and Fantini, for instance. However, instead of the nonstop series of surprise raids which Derry feared, Colonel Kappler took his revenge in a manner comparable only with the horror of Lidice. For every dead German, 10 people, 320 in all, were selected for slaughter. Taken from the various prisons in the city and from the Via Tasso and Via Principe Amedeo headquarters, they included political prisoners and prostitutes, petty thieves, recaptured escapers, *padrones*, all chosen quite indiscriminately.

With their hands tied behind their backs, none in doubt of their fate, they were marched through silent streets to a point near the outskirts of the city where they were thrust into trucks and driven to the Ardeatine Caves at Domitilla. Here, still bound, they were pushed in batches into the caves and mown down by machine-gun fire. For hours the massacre continued, until Kappler gave the order and the mined entrances to the caves were blown and the dead, and still living, were entombed behind hundreds of tons of rock. Among the 320 were 5 of the organization's helpers, including the gallant radio operator and saboteur Umberto Losena.

As Rome, indeed all Italy, seethed at the out-and-out barbarity of the reprisal, hundreds of previously uncommitted people rallied to whatever Allied cause they could best help, but the Germans brought another two thousand SS and other troops into the city and now launched the series of raids and countermeasures Derry had expected. The Ardeatine Massacre more than cancelled out the ill-feeling caused by the bombing of Monte Cassino—it was as big a psychological error as the German persecution of the Jews at the beginning of the occupation. Now the Germans, and especially Koch's gang of thugs, answerable to no military control and compared bitterly and not inaccurately by O'Flaherty to the Black and Tans—made all movement on the streets after curfew practically impossible, shooting first and asking any questions later. Derry discussed with O'Flaherty a plan to hide all the escapers in the catacombs which had sheltered thousands of the early Christians from the pagan emperors centuries before. It was all worked out in detail, every billet being told how to get into the maze of subterranean tunnels (and how to avoid getting lost in them), but it never proved necessary to put the plan into operation.

Over in the American College, Colin Lesslie made up his mind that, whatever happened, he was not going to be recaptured now. He suddenly developed a passion for gardening—after all, spring was here—and he constructed a cleverly camouflaged dugout in which he could hide, if by any chance the College were raided. He also excavated enough hideouts under the flower beds for all the people living in the granary should it ever become necessary.

As the Germans and Fascists stepped up their attacks and as the full implications of the Ardeatine horror seeped in, the escape organization found that scores of people who previously had steered carefully clear of any association with them were now only too anxious to help, nor were they concerned with payment for their services. They would do anything to assist the Allied cause, even with the knowledge that execution was the price of capture. Their help was sorely needed in providing new billets in a hurry because, during the first few days of April, the Germans and Fascists scored a whole series of successes, mainly due to Perfetti.

Furman was living with the clerk, Romeo Giuliani, and the teenage son Gino. One day, quite casually, Gino told Furman that he knew Perfetti. Furman instantly left the billet and stayed elsewhere for a few nights. When, however, nothing happened, he returned to the Giuliani home on April 5, but on the night of April 7 he went to an all-night party on the other side of the city. That was how he happened to be absent when the Fascists arrived and arrested both father and son. Romeo was released, but the boy was held and "cracked" in the hands of Koch. Furman got hold of Joe Pollak and they set out to make a round of billets to warn the inhabitants. The idea of going together was that if one walked into a trap in an apartment, the other would be able to get away and report to Derry. Of all the billets known to Gino, only two escaped a raid. Simpson, not knowing of the Gino disaster, had gone to the basement apartment near the Vatican itself where O'Flaherty was sending all new arrivals, to find that the *padrone*, Paolini, had been arrested, but not before he had been able to hide five escapers in the cellar, pushing his bed over the trap-door. Furman sent in a long list of recaptured prisoners, mentioning that he had managed to save two men only. Within a day or so even this couple were caught. Derry noticed with dismay that the raided billets were getting closer and closer to the Chevalier's apartment and sent a note to both Simpson and Furman warning them to keep away from it as much as possible.

Simpson never received this warning. He simply vanished.

He had been arrested on the night of April 18 while spending the night with an American, Lieutenant Dukate, in the home of two Italian black market operators. The Fascists knew exactly who they had come for and left the black marketeers alone, taking only Dukate and Simpson. Everything the organization could do to locate Simpson failed. Giuseppe could get no line on him, Molly Stanley could learn nothing at the Regina Coeli, diplomatic inquiries by the Swiss got nowhere and even a rather theatrical approach by the glamorous film actress Flora Volpini, in whose apartment both Simpson and Furman had stayed at various times, failed. She went to the Italian governor of the Regina Coeli, an old friend, but he said he had no knowledge of any Lieutenant Simpson. And indeed neither had he, for Simpson never used his real name and the Germans never learned it. Which caused a lot of trouble later.

While O'Flaherty and Derry were inclined to blame Perfetti also for Simpson's arrest, it was in fact a case of *cherchez la femme*! Lieutenant Dukate, like many others at the time, had quite a few girlfriends in Rome. When he began to see less of one of them named Carla and rather more of a new girl, Carla went straight to Koch and told him about her American former boyfriend and of the English soldier staying with him. Koch was jubilant at the double capture and was, for him, in a good mood when a few hours later Father Roche, a priest from St. Patrick's Augustinian Church and one of O'Flaherty's hardest workers, was brought before him. Koch, who had publicly said of O'Flaherty, "I'll have the nails off his fingers before shooting him", had no idea that Father Roche had any association with the Monsignor, for the priest had been arrested only for a small act of charity. To impress the Romans with their success in holding the Cassino line, the Germans made a practice of parading captured Allied prisoners through the streets. As one such column passed St. Patrick's, Father Roche stepped out into the road and handed cigarettes to the soldiers.

Koch snarled viciously when Father Roche was brought before him—but not at the priest. "Go and get me some real criminals", he yelled. "I want throwers of bombs, not of cigarettes. Stick this priest in the Regina Coeli to cool off!" Father Roche was released after three days.

The Germans next made two other moves. They brought strong diplomatic pressure to bear on the Swiss Government and all aid from the Swiss Legation ceased. The Swiss had been warned that the Germans knew perfectly well they were assisting escaped Allied prisoners-of-war and if this continued for a day longer the member of the Legation staff most involved, Captain Trippi, would be arrested. Then, through Baron von Weiszacker, they made representations to the heads of some of the religious orders in Rome, which resulted in Fathers Borg, Madden and Buckley being confined to their houses. The Germans also secured the closure by the Vatican authorities of all outside approaches to the Collegio Teutonicum. O'Flaherty's room was out of bounds. With over 3,900 men currently under their care, with 8 escapers shot in the country and 40 others recaptured inside a month, O'Flaherty and Derry were at last on the defensive. They had a further shock with one of the narrowest escapes of all, of the men only just moved out of the Chevalier apartment. These five soldiers were now billeted with an Italian named Giovanni and all were in when the Fascists arrived, hammering at the door. There was no other way out of the apartment and in despair Giovanni thrust the five out onto the tiny balcony at the rear and pulled the curtain across the window. The Fascists found nothing incriminating in the apartment and were about to leave when their sergeant pointed to the curtained window and said, "What's behind there?"

"Only the balcony, the usual thing, you know", said Giovanni, starting to pour sweat. "Would you like a drink now you're finished?"

"Certainly," said the sergeant, "as soon as I have checked the balcony!"

Giovanni stood trembling as the sergeant stepped out onto the balcony and gazed around. There was utter silence. The sergeant returned to the room. "Not much of a view to these apartments, is there?" he remarked pleasantly. "And now, what about that drink?"

Unable to speak, Giovanni poured drinks for the Fascists and waited while they finished the bottle. As the door closed behind them he dashed for the balcony and peered down to the courtyard. It was empty. Puzzled but relieved, he was about to get back into the room when he heard a sibilant whisper from over his head. Looking up, he saw a ladder being lowered from the balcony on the floor above. One by one the five men descended, saved by the fact that Giovanni kept his stepladder on his balcony because it took up too much room in the kitchen.

As if Derry had not enough on his shoulders, quite a number of the escapers themselves were giving trouble. True, they had been cooped up for weeks, in some cases months, and were restless. They tried to relieve the monotony by staging parties in different billets, moving on from one to the other; the bolder went to cafes and restaurants and drew from Baron von Weiszacker the sharp complaint to the Vatican and to Sir D'Arcy Osborne that the British were so generous to escaped prisoners-of-war they could afford to drink in the best places! There were several awkward cases of drunkenness and Derry had to drop down hard on the whole setup. On April 23 he issued a general order to the top men, code-listed: "Golf, Eyerish, John, Fanny, Horace, Mr. Bishop, Sandro, Spike, Emma, Dutchpa, Sailor and Rinso." This pointed out that the current expectation in Rome was that the Allies would not arrive before the autumn and that in the meantime the Germans would do everything in their power to round up every single POW. In view of this difficult situation and the cases of indiscipline, Derry continued, no more escapers were to be billeted in Rome and any that did arrive were to be given money and sent back to the country. Billet parties would cease. In selected cases the allowance of six thousand lire per man for the month of May was not to be handed over to escapers in one lump sum but in installments so that it would be spent on food and lodging instead of on liquor.

When Derry showed O'Flaherty these instructions he was surprised, not only that the Monsignor did not demur at a tougher line with the men (for he was all for giving them as much freedom and comfort as possible), but that he seemed unusually subdued.

"What's troubling you, Monsignor?" Derry asked eventually.

"This sort of thing, me boy", replied O'Flaherty, handing over a letter. It was one of four brought to him by a priest from the country who had performed the last rites for four British escaped prisoners-of-war who had been recaptured by the Germans and shot.

The letter read:

"Dear Mother and Father and Family,

"This is the last letter I will be able to write as I get shot today. Dear family, I have laid down my life for my country and everything that was dear to me. I hope this war will be over soon so that you will all have peace for ever. Goodbye.

"Your ever loving soldier son and brother."

There were tears in O'Flaherty's eyes and Derry was not far from them either as he went through the letters one by one. When Derry had finished reading, the two men looked at one another for a wordless second or two. O'Flaherty's mouth thinned as he took the letters back. "I will see that these are passed on", he said. "It is more important than ever that we save every man we can, *whatever the risk*."

CHAPTER FOURTEEN

"Quando Vengono?"

As the April days passed, punctuated by bomb explosions and the occasional killing of an SS or Fascist Gestapo man, general dislocation of transport and supplies placed an even heavier burden on O'Flaherty and particularly those of his priests who could still move about. A number of the *padrones* were no longer able to get black market food supplies or extras from the countryside and were forced to ask the organization to transfer escapers to other billets where, perhaps, they could be fed. The task of finding new billets might have been greater but for the bitter anti-German attitude and even more now the general feeling that "something" was in the air. *Quando vengono?* ("When are they coming?") was the question on everyone's lips. The answer came on May 12, when the Allies opened their big offensive on the southern front.

Derry in the British Legation, Furman in his billet and hundreds of the priests in their monasteries heard the news over the B.B.C. Radio and responded, not only with impromptu little celebrations but with new security moves. Derry was afraid that the jubilant escapers might now do things *really* indiscreet. Everyone was told to stay strictly indoors for a few days at least and to build up a stock of food and water in each billet so that they could stand a short siege if necessary, or if it became absolutely impossible to deliver supplies during the actual recapture of the city. But some of the escapers simply would not obey orders and two of them, a man named Martin and an American sergeant named Everett decided, of all things, to visit Mrs. Chevalier and get a good meal!

There were no longer any soldiers billetted in the Chevalier apartment, but it functioned still as a temporary clearing house for a few hours on occasions and as a general base for food distribution. By now even Mrs. Chevalier's nerves were overstrained by the months of tension (in fact her health was permanently damaged by it all), and the little apartment on Via dell' Impero was no longer the cheery place it once had been. Mother and daughters were all too conscious of the tobacco shop across the street, where now there were two Germans in plain clothes, though they hardly bothered to conceal their pistols, and an Italian woman worked with them.

On the day the Allied offensive started, the two Germans strolled across the street for the first time, so far as the Chevaliers had noticed, and questioned Egidio, the block porter, about the inhabitants of apartment nine. Egidio gave as little information as possible and sent Elvira upstairs to warn Mrs. Chevalier. She at once made one of her rare telephone calls to O'Flaherty, warning him that she was now under full-time observation. A message was rushed to Furman to tell all escapers who knew Mrs. Chevalier to stay away from her apartment. Presumably Martin and Everett did not get this warning, but in any event they were flagrantly disobeying Derry's orders when the next day they turned up at the apartment, watched as they entered by the two SS men, while the Italian woman hastily got on the telephone to Via Tasso.

Half-fearfully opening her door to the gentle knock of the two visitors, Mrs. Chevalier gaped at them for a moment. Then, "Go away . . . run!" she hissed. "The Germans are watching at this minute. Go!" And she slammed the door shut. Martin and Everett were well aware that to go down the stairs now would most likely mean their arrest, and probably death in the mood the Germans were in. But they knew their first duty was to protect "Mrs. M" and unhesitatingly they started down the three stone flights. Reaching the street, they saw the two Germans come out of the tobacco shop and wait to let some traffic pass before starting to cross the road. Martin and Everett broke into a run, dived into a narrow alley and into the back courtyard of a block of apartments. From here they were able to get out into a parallel street and make good their escape.

Meanwhile Mrs. Chevalier, ice-cool in the emergency, was putting her final escape plan into operation. One by one her daughters, leaving everything behind them except their handbags, went down the stairs and out into the street and walked away in different directions. Mrs. Chevalier came down last, fully expecting to be arrested at the main door. But the two SS men were still combing the alleys and the Italian woman saw nothing suspicious in women coming out of a block where there was constant coming and going all day. One by one again the girls assembled at a home of a friend on the far side of the city, and in a day or two they were moved out of Rome entirely, to a farm where they stayed until after the liberation. Now, however, Kappler made an important capture.

"Look at this diagram . . . look well . . . and tell us just exactly where you fit into it. We know you are an English spy, you see, and we know pretty well all about your organization. You have the choice—tell us all, or you die . . . tonight!"

The almost-naked priest stared down in horror at the diagram, realizing that Colonel Kappler's SS men had in their hands a very nearly accurate picture of the O'Flaherty escape organization. And he himself, if he broke under torture, could provide the most vital information to fill in the gaps. Father Anselmo Musters, whose code name was "Dutchpa" because he came from Holland, had been one of O'Flaherty's earliest recruits and his arrest—the arrest of any priest—by the SS was perhaps the thing O'Flaherty and Derry most dreaded. Now it had happened.

Father Musters was making his rounds of the billets in his care, handing out the May cash allowances, and he had just left a South African sergeant when he sensed that he was being followed. A large, tough-looking man in plain clothes but unmistakably SS, was keeping step a few paces behind him. Father Musters abandoned his intention of going on to the next billet on his list and started across the piazza to enter the great Basilica of St. Mary Major, or St. Mary of the Snows. He calculated that if could reach the steps that run across the front of the church, he would be on extraterritorial ground and the SS man might give up. But the SS man increased his pace, got in front of the priest, and halted him just by the tall column carrying a bronze statue of the Madonna and Child near the foot of the steps.

"Identity documents!" he demanded—and these Father Musters did not have.

Cunningly, the priest said, "I will show them to you on the steps of the church", and pressed past the SS man and onto the first steps. The SS man again tried to bar his way, but Father Musters dodged to one side and started up the side steps that led to the five huge doors of the Basilica. Pulling his pistol, the SS man followed, calling to the priest to stop. Father Musters paused, glanced quickly at the gun, then turned and continued to the top. As he crossed to one of the doors into the atrium he felt a heavy blow on the back of his head and collapsed forward, half in and half out of the door. A Palatine Guard rushed forward from within the church and dragged Father Musters inside. The SS man stood for a few seconds outside the door, glaring impotently, then thrust his pistol back into his pocket and ran down the steps and away.

When he had recovered enough, Father Musters telephoned O'Flaherty and told him what had happened. "Stay in St. Mary Major tonight," said the Monsignor, "and we will collect you in the morning. You will be quite safe in the church." O'Flaherty was wrong. He had underrated the German's determination to capture a man he was sure was an English officer masquerading as a priest.

Only a few minutes after Father Musters had settled down to rest in the sacristy on the right-hand side of the Basilica, a squad of SS men, heavily armed, surrounded the area and closed in on the church. Six of them, led by an SS captain, mounted the steps, shoved the Palatine Guard aside, and clumped across the marble floor, between an avenue of columns of shining white marble from Mount Hymetus outside Athens, and into the sacristy.

"Come with us", said the captain. "You are under arrest."

"But this is extraterritorial property", replied "Dutchpa". "You have no right to enter here. I have been ordered by my religious superiors to stay here until they fetch me."

"Your 'religious superiors'!" scoffed the captain. "You mean the English spy ring. Now get up, and come—at once."

"I will not move from here", said the priest quietly.

The SS captain turned to one of his men and snatched a submachine gun from him. Turning back to Father Musters he took careful aim and swung the heavy weapon with full force across the side of the priest's head.

Father Musters fell out of his chair onto the floor, barely conscious. Two SS men took him by the feet and dragged him the length of the church, out and down the long flight of steps, his head banging on each step as they descended. He was still only semiconscious when taken into a room at the Via Tasso headquarters of the SS, but he was aware of a strong exultation among the Germans. From their conversation he gathered that they were quite convinced they had captured an English colonel in disguise. To Father Musters it was uncomfortably clear also that the SS men knew that some English officer was helping O'Flaherty run the organization and that this officer had in the past disguised himself as a priest. It was of course Sam Derry they were thinking of.

Father Musters was too weak to strip himself when ordered, and the SS men more or less tore his clothes from him. Linings were ripped out and seams opened up, even his shoes were cut completely to pieces. His arms were handcuffed behind him and his feet bound with a chain. For hours he was interrogated by the Gestapo, beaten from head to foot, threatened with obscene tortures, promised his life if he would talk, guaranteed a horrible death if he would not. "Dutchpa", inwardly praying all the time for strength to resist, said nothing. This questioning was to continue for three ghastly weeks, while the Vatican authorities tried unavailingly to secure his release, and Derry cleared out every billet known to the captured priest.

On the twenty-first day even the masters of torture and interrogation gave in. Father Musters was put in a pitch-black cell in the basement and kept in total isolation for another fortnight, then put on a train for Germany, a con-

centration camp, and probable death. But the priest was
indeed made of stern stuff, of true Dutch courage and
determination. The train halted in a siding at Florence for
some hours. Freed of his handcuffs to eat, Father Musters
was left alone in the carriage for a few moments. He squeezed
out through the window, jumped onto the tracks and was
away before the guards knew what had happened. He
returned at once to Rome, but by then the capital had been
freed and the Via Tasso held no menace for anyone any
more.

A day or two after Father Musters had been taken, Lieutenant Furman very nearly joined him at Via Tasso. He was
moving from billet to billet with money for the *padrones*,
and also on this occasion some packets of American tobacco
captured by the Germans and sold by them on the Rome
black market. This morning Furman's pockets were bulging with tobacco. In his breast pocket was his notebook
with the coded accounts of money disbursed. Under his
lapel he wore a tiny Union Jack brooch as a lucky charm.
The packed streetcar on which he was travelling was stopped
in one of the SS "blitz" raids. The streetcar was completely
surrounded by soldiers and others formed a corridor leading from the streetcar to a block of apartments, which obviously was going to be employed as an interrogation center.
As the driver opened the doors at each end of the streetcar,
an SS officer and two troopers entered at one end. Women
and children were told to stay where they were, all the men
were to leave by the front door. Furman was standing near
the front exit and now the press of men moving forward
threatened to push him out into the arms of the waiting
soldiers. Luckily an Italian man rose from his seat at this
moment, pushing ahead of Furman, who dropped down
into the vacated seat, beside a woman who was clutching a

shopping bag on her knees. The woman looked understandably startled as Furman pulled his notebook from his pocket and tore out the incriminating pages, crushing them into a small ball. Shaking her head in silent amazement, the woman glanced away and in that instant Furman dropped the ball of paper into her basket. He then got up and made his way out of the streetcar, almost the last man to leave.

About forty prisoners were assembled in the central courtyard of the apartments. Furman was third from the end of the line which moved slowly forward to where two officers of the Italian Republican Army were checking identity papers. Furman's immediate anxiety was to get rid of his four telltale packets of American tobacco. He had to take each one furtively out of his pocket, break the tough covering paper, empty the tobacco into his pocket and crumple up the wrappings and drop them underfoot. Meanwhile he was watching the behavior of the prisoners being questioned. Most of them protested angrily, demanding to be released instantly, some claiming to be "loyal Fascists", others boasting hopefully of their friendship with powerful officials and the like. It did no good whatever for most of them. By the time Furman reached the head of the line only five men had been released, the rest being pushed into the main building, where one room was being used as a temporary prison.

When it came to Furman's turn he handed over his papers calmly, without saying a word. It was only then that he remembered the Union Jack badge under his lapel. There was nothing he could do about it now. He watched the Army officer studying his identity card—one of those which was a perfectly genuine one in a sense, like Derry's that the organization had tricked the German Minister into signing. With the identity card was a document forged by Princess

Pallavicini and May certifying that Luigi Bianchi, born in Padua in 1909, a bachelor, was a Vatican employee in the Office of Technical Services. The examining officer called over his superior and showed him the documents. There was some whispering—Furman stood haughtily silent.

The senior officer started to walk toward Furman, obviously about to question him. Furman smiled disdainfully at him and the officer halted. Impetuously he handed the documents to his junior who passed them over to Furman and said curtly, "All right. Go." He then saluted. Furman put the papers very deliberately back in his pocket, then strolled slowly back down the line of soldiers to the street outside. Once round the corner he had to lean against a wall, weak with sheer relief. Then he took to his heels and ran as he had never run before.

With the fall of Cassino on May 18, all Italy was at last certain that the Allies would win. The Germans had not much doubt about that either, as Blon Kiernan was able to report after another of her tea-time chats with Prince Bismarck. Now, as Derry recorded, "everyone who knew anything at all about the organization was falling head over heels to join it and get on the bandwagon!" Way ahead of them all in sudden new helpfulness was the double agent Cipolla. Sources of information that had in the past been firmly closed were now opening everywhere, and at last Furman managed to discover that Simpson was alive, though in Regina Coeli, together with the American, Dukate. The big fear in the minds of all connected with the organization was that the Germans, in one last furious outburst, would start to shift all the prisoners out of Rome and to concentration camps or even shoot them. O'Flaherty, Derry, Furman and Adrienne and Renzo Lucidi had anxious conferences to see how Simpson could be got out of Regina

Coeli and, eventually, it was the woman's brain that came up with a possible answer.

"The Germans trust Cipolla completely", she said. "He told me that he is to be left behind with a radio transmitter and plenty of money when they evacuate the city. What he wants above all is to be in the good books of the Allies when they get here. We can give him his chance. All he has to do is tell the Germans that he has made contact with the British spy ring, as they call it, and that he will be able to infiltrate it and work with it if he can get Simpson released as an earnest of good faith. The Germans surely will fall for that."

It was decided that Cipolla should ask simply for the release of two prisoners of his choice. Without giving the game away completely, he could not indicate that he knew of any particular arrested officer. He was, however, told by Adrienne, on Derry's instructions, to do his best to secure the release of Simpson and a Captain John Armstrong who had been in the prison for about nine months. Armstrong had nothing whatever to do with the escape organization. The Germans agreed at once and gave Cipolla a list of British prisoners in Regina Coeli. When he studied this, Cipolla could find neither of the names he wanted. He had no alternative but to pick two men at random and, greatly to their pleased surprise, two English civilians who had been jailed since Italy entered the war found themselves free.

This trick could not be used a second time and Derry now discovered from Blon Kiernan that the Germans had been making inquiries at the Irish Legation about an Irishman named "William O'Flynn" who was supposed to be working at the Vatican. The Legation replied, in all truth, that they knew nothing about him. "William O'Flynn" was Simpson's alias, and it was under this name that he was now held in a special wing at Regina Coeli, a section guarded exclusively by Germans. Even Molly Stanley could make no contact with him there.

But somehow Simpson managed to smuggle out a letter, probably through the barber, Messina, and this took a fortnight to reach O'Flaherty and Derry. Simpson reported that he had been in prison for three weeks but had not once been interrogated. He had given the "William O'Flynn" name. He asked for ten thousand lire, to be used by himself and others if the opportunity arose. Derry sent the money and a warning that the O'Flynn alias had been broken by the Germans. Neither money nor message ever got through.

CHAPTER FIFTEEN

The Enemy Pleads for Aid

INSTEAD THERE WAS a quite astonishing development. O'Flaherty was at work in the Holy Office one morning when he was told an unnamed Roman nobleman wished to see him. The man was brought to his room.

"We have never met, Monsignor," he began, "but you were responsible for saving a certain girl's life. Do you remember, you made her a 'temporary member' of the Swiss Guard?"

O'Flaherty grinned for he remembered very well indeed. The girl, daughter of the Duchess Colerina Cesaro and known for her anti-Fascist views, was being sought by Koch's men and contacted O'Flaherty. She was told to come to the Bernini Colonnade just before the midnight guard-changing ceremony. Here, standing well back in the deep shadows were O'Flaherty, Derry and May. May had a Swiss Guard uniform, covered by a cloak, over his arm. The three men stood in a semicircle with their backs to the girl while she shed her dress and scrambled into the uniform. As the relieved guards began to march back to the Arco delle Campane, she slipped out of the shadows and attached herself to the rear of the small column. Meanwhile O'Flaherty had gone back into the Vatican and, as the column passed through the inner courtyard, a huge hand came out of a doorway to grab the girl by the shoulder and draw her away into the

German cemetery and thence into the Collegio itself. Here she pulled off the uniform and put on a raincoat, provided by May, and May and Derry then escorted her to the British Legation where she stayed, officially at least, unknown to Sir D'Arcy, until she could be given sanctuary in one of the South American Legations in Rome.

It was clear that the visitor wanted something of the Monsignor. O'Flaherty asked politely about the girl and then the nobleman paused.

"Er ... this is a little delicate, Monsignor", he began.

"We are used to delicate situations here", replied O'Flaherty smoothly. "What can I do for you?"

But even O'Flaherty was shaken when his caller started to explain.

"I have come to you from one of your mortal enemies, Monsignor", he said. "From Ludwig Koch!"

O'Flaherty blinked at him but said nothing. Was this another trap? The nobleman went on, "Koch, as you will know, is now in sole charge of all recaptured escapers in the Regina Coeli—including quite a few of your people. Now he is most understandably afraid of what might happen when the Allies reach Rome. He is not alone in that, but perhaps he has more to fear than most ... if some of his victims ever got their hands on him ... I need not elaborate. And, believe me, Monsignor, I would not take up your time by coming to you, even though you are a priest, to plead for Koch. He thinks he can get away quietly to the north, but he can't take his wife and mother, and seemingly even that inhuman man has some feelings. He wants *you* to save them!"

O'Flaherty rose from his desk and paced his small room for a moment or two. "It is", he said, "not for me to judge Koch or anyone else, and I will certainly help as I would help anyone in trouble if I could. But Koch must also assist me, or rather others. He must do all in his power to prevent further loss of life. . . ."

"Ah, Monsignor," the nobleman broke in, "Koch has thought of that! He says that if you will safeguard his wife and mother, he will make sure that all your friends are left behind in Regina Coeli instead of being transported to Germany."

O'Flaherty had no faith in Koch's word and said so. "His offer is not enough. Please tell him from me that if he first frees and delivers safely to me Lieutenant Simpson and Captain Armstrong, who are in the prison, then I will make the necessary arrangements for his relatives."

Spurred on no doubt by the rumble of gunfire that was almost continuous as the Allies pressed on toward Rome, Koch moved swiftly. Within hours Simpson, sitting in his cell in Regina Coeli, heard a call for "Lieutenant Simpson" on the prison loudspeaker system. But he had not received Derry's message and was still sticking to his story that he was William O'Flynn. This was a trap he was not going to fall into. Nor did Captain Armstrong answer to his name.

When the nobleman came back to report failure to O'Flaherty, the Monsignor had to make up his mind to choose between two dangerous courses. Simpson faced death if left in the prison, since the Germans already knew that "William O'Flynn" was an alias. On the other hand, to tell Koch, of all people, of the deception, proving "O'Flynn's" connection with the organization, could be an equally certain death warrant for Simpson, if Koch wished to play false, if the whole story was in fact a trap.

The Monsignor muttered a quick prayer for guidance, then said, "All right. Tell Koch that Simpson is to be found under the name of William O'Flynn. I do not know what name Captain Armstrong may be using."

Koch was given this message, but events were now moving too fast. On June 3 May went to Derry's office and told him that a British armored spearhead had reached the Pope's villa at Castel Gandolfo and that the officer in charge was calling the Vatican by radio. Derry rushed to take over from the Vatican Radio operator and gave the tank commander a detailed account of the military situation in Rome so far as he knew it, telling him of the location of German anti-tank guns, for example. The tank officer was, in his turn, able to tell Derry that Valmontone, the military key to the capital, had just fallen. Liberation could be only hours away.

Amid the now constant boom of the guns, the Germans started to pull out. Nazi troops on prison duty were withdrawn, and the Italian guards simply fled. At Regina Coeli the prisoners took over and began to release themselves in an orderly fashion. First to leave were those who lived in the neighborhood, then came Allied ex-prisoners-of-war, including Simpson.

Simpson's actions on gaining his freedom were utterly typical of his unselfishness and sense of duty and discipline. He gathered around him as many of the escapers as he could and, under the noses of the Germans still swarming in the streets, shepherded them through the city to billet after billet until all were accommodated for the night. Only then did he think of shelter for himself.

Furman and Renzo Lucidi were working on their billeting accounts that night when the doorbell rang sharply. And again, then once more. The two men jumped to their feet in alarm. For this was the secret signal that had been discarded by the organization after Perfetti had passed it to the Germans! They listened anxiously as Peppina opened the door. There was a loud, piercing scream, and they dashed for the hall. But it was a scream of joy. There stood Bill Simpson with both Adrienne and Peppina hugging and kissing him.

As soon as Koch's emissary had left his office, O'Flaherty had set about making arrangements for the safety of the wife and mother of the Torturer of Rome. They were to be taken to Naples and given shelter in a convent. But when a message was sent to them, they both refused, insisting they would go north in the hope of catching up with Koch, who had got away sometime on June 1 or 2. The Fascist had, however, been as good as his word. About seventy people, including all known to be Allied escapers, were left behind in Regina Coeli, but a small group *was* taken away as one last vicious gesture and bundled on a truck to accompany the German troops northwards—for fourteen miles. There, by the roadside, they were shot. Among the bodies was that of Captain Armstrong, the man the organization had tried so hard to save.

For very good reasons indeed, some of the most worried people in Rome at this moment were the Russians. There were more than four hundred escaped Russian prisoners-of-war hidden in Rome, some placed by O'Flaherty in the Russian College near the Basilica of St. Mary Major, others in private billets, generally with Communist *padrones*, for although O'Flaherty, as he told Derry, considered Communism infinitely worse than Nazism (or even the Black and Tans), he had no scruples about using Reds if it saved even one life. And the Germans would have no mercy on any Russians they caught.

Early on the morning of Saturday, June 3, while Derry was talking to the British tank commander at Castel Gandolfo, a student from the Russian College went to the Jesuit generalate, practically in the shadow of the Bernini

Colonnade, and asked to see Father Francis Joy, S.J. (later Rector of Clongowes, Ireland's foremost Jesuit College). Father Joy knew O'Flaherty well—both were Kerrymen and O'Flaherty had been trained at the Jesuit Mungret College—but had never so far had anything to do with the organization. He was, in fact, working in Rome on an Anti-Communist Secretariat, established by his Order to fight world Communism. The student explained that while the escapers hidden in the Russian College were probably safe enough, those in scattered billets could be picked up any minute if the Germans made one last frantic, vengeful drive. It was proposed therefore to move every one of them to new hiding places. Before this could be done, the current *padrones* would have to be paid off, since a resentful one might well tell the Germans what was happening. The Russians, however, had no money.

"If you will wait here," said Father Joy, "I think I may be able to help you."

The Jesuit went directly to O'Flaherty in the Holy Office. As the main doors to the street were closed, he had to go through the Arco delle Campane and past the Swiss Guards, but was admitted without difficulty. He related the Russian's problem and O'Flaherty said, "Of course we must help them, Francis. Stay here a moment...."

Hurrying across to the British Legation, O'Flaherty found Derry back in his little room. "Have you got any cash about, me boy?" he asked. "I've a wee problem. We want to shift some Russians to make sure the Germans don't get 'em, but the landladies want their money first!"

Grinning, Derry produced 120,000 in lire. "I hope Joe Stalin pays it back!" he said.

Throughout that gloriously sunny June Saturday and Sunday in Rome, as the Germans pulled out in long columns and the Allied guns were at last silent, the Russians were switched to new hideouts—just in case. It was an unreal two days. As the hours passed the Germans just crumpled. Disorderly bands of them roamed the streets, dangerous to the last, jeering at the more fortunate of their troops who had managed to get hold of trucks to carry them away, yet still stopping passersby at gunpoint to demand identity papers! Early on Saturday evening Furman had one last brush with a tired, unshaven and unkempt German officer who stopped him on the corner of Via Salaria, the main evacuation route to the north.

"Why are you out in the street? There is a curfew!" said the German, prodding Furman's ribs with a pistol.

"I am just going home. I was delayed", said Furman placatingly.

"Run ... run ... let me see you run", snarled the officer, but wearily.

As Furman told the story later, "I was damned if I was going to run for any Jerry now!" He walked on slowly, not knowing if he would get a bullet in his back.

At 7:15 P.M. on Sunday, June 4, the head of the American Eighty-eighth Division entered the Piazza Venezia in the heart of Rome, French troops started to march along the Via dell' Impero, where once the Chevaliers had lived, and the British moved up the Via Nazionale, led by Scottish pipers. Across the Tiber the sound of the pipes reached St. Peter's.

Pope Pius heard the triumphant skirl through the wide open windows of his study. Five men stood on the roof of the Hospice Santa Marta, bathed in the evening sunlight, watching the victorious lines of troops and tanks and guns flow into the Eternal City. There was Sir D'Arcy Osborne, Hugh Montgomery, Father Owen Sneddon, Major Sam

Derry and John May. For a while they gazed across Rome
in silence, then suddenly all reserve went—they burst out
cheering, shaking hands, slapping one another on the back,
laughing almost hysterically, on the verge of tears. And, as
they watched, the enormous square of St. Peter's began fill-
ing up, one moment an empty expanse, the next dotted with
tiny black ants, then completely covered as thousands and
thousands poured in, cheering also, yelling, weeping, dancing and leaping with joy. As at a signal, what seemed to be
the bells of every one of the four hundred churches of
Rome began to peal out, almost overwhelmingly. British and
American flags, long carefully stowed away, appeared at every
window in sight, escapers and evaders came out of their hiding places, everyone, it seemed, converging on St. Peter's
Square. Rose petals showered down from building tops, a
vast hum of excitement, of gratitude, filled the air. Then,
suddenly, there was total silence. The five men on the roof-
top switched their eyes down to their left, the uncountable
thousands in the piazza lifted their eyes up to the balcony on
which Pope Pius had appeared alone in plain white cassock.

    The silence seemed to last for an eternity, then with break-
ing voice the Pope spoke. "In the days just past we trem-
bled for Rome. Today we give thanks to God that both
contending armies have collaborated to preserve the Eternal City." Then he gave his blessing, "To the City and to
the World" and once more the piazza dissolved into a seeth-
ing mass of dancing, singing, cheering people. On the Hospice roof May spoke softly. "We do have some extremely
good champagne downstairs, gentlemen." Quietly now,
slightly dazed with emotion, everyone followed Sir D'Arcy
down to the British Legation.

    Down in the streets of Rome, Furman was wandering
about in a sort of delirious delight; Simpson and the Lucidis

were arranging a colossal party that would not be interrupted by the crash of SS rifle butts on the door; Father Musters, bruised but indomitable, was hitchhiking from Florence; the Chevalier family were celebrating in their farmhouse refuge.

Hugh Joseph O'Flaherty was on his knees in the tiny chapel on the ground floor of the Hospice Santa Marta, praying for guidance in the colossal task that now lay ahead of him. From henceforth, since the Allies were no longer the underdogs, O'Flaherty almost lost interest in them. They no longer needed his help, except in minor matters, but the Germans and Fascists did.

It was his former enemies who, charity ordained, must be helped. O'Flaherty meant it and proved it when he said that he would always help anyone in distress, whoever, whatever they were, or had been. Pope Pius himself knew this. Cardinal Ottaviani, the stern disciplinarian of the Holy Office and O'Flaherty's direct superior, knew it also. It was the only reason they kept their eyes so tightly closed to the activities of their obstreperous Irish Monsignor.

CHAPTER SIXTEEN

Rewards and Retributions

AT THE LIBERATION of Rome the organization was caring for 3,925 escapers and men who had succeeded in evading arrest. Of these 1,695 were British, 896 South African, 429 Russian, 425 Greek, 185 American, and the rest from 20 different countries. Not counted were the Jews and sundry other men and women in O'Flaherty's strictly personal care.

O'Flaherty was immediately immersed in his work for Italians and Germans and Derry found himself appointed a temporary military attaché to the Holy See, to liaise between the Allied Military Government of Rome and Sir D'Arcy Osborne. Within days of the liberation General Alexander, commander in chief Allied Armies in Italy, had arrived in Rome and sent for Derry. The commander in chief already knew a great deal about Monsignor O'Flaherty because, an Irish Guardsman himself, he had given orders that if any Irish Guards officer escapers were found, they should report to him at his headquarters at Caserta. There was only one— Lieutenant Colin Lesslie, whom O'Flaherty had hidden in the American College. While Lesslie was incarcerated here and Grenadier Guards Lieutenant Paul Freyberg was interned in the Vatican, O'Flaherty had arranged for May to carry letters between the two men. As soon as Paul Freyberg learned that his father, General Freyberg, was coming in a staff car to fetch him from the Vatican, Lesslie was brought down from the American College and taken in the general's car to First Army Headquarters at Valmontone, where he was ordered to go and see the Commander in Chief. Alexander kept Lesslie for two days at his house before sending him back to rejoin his regiment in England, and during that time Lesslie told him everything he knew about the fantastic Irish Monsignor.

General Alexander was intrigued and impressed, even more so after hearing Derry's account, and he was to prove a powerful friend to O'Flaherty in his new work of mercy. Derry was asked if he would stay on in Rome and organize an Allied Screening, or Claims, Commission, to deal with the tens of thousands of applications from people who had helped the Allies, more especially through the escape organization. Furman had already commandeered an office for them, the ground floor of the block of apartments in Via Scialoia where the Lucidis lived, and he and Simpson had hidden at different times. Captain Byrnes dug up his biscuit boxes from the Vatican gardens and Derry, Simpson, Furman, Byrnes and the Greek, Theodore Meletiou, began their enormous task of receiving and sifting claims. As for the escapers themselves, responsibility for them was handed over to a special Repatriation Unit. Among the civilian staff recruited for the Screening Commission as its work grew was Gemma Chevalier, while her mother found work at the reopened British Embassy. A year after the liberation Monsignor O'Flaherty married Gemma to Corporal Kenneth Sands of the Hampshire Regiment, who had been attached to the Commission.

O'Flaherty's small ground floor room in the Holy Office was now busier than it had ever been. Thousands of Italians were prisoners-of-war, mainly in South Africa, and their relatives swarmed to the Holy Office to get news of them;

hundreds more Italians called on O'Flaherty to claim recompense for money they had (or had not) spent to help the Allies, and these he referred to Derry. This work was to occupy him for years and he began it with typical energy. He decided that he would have to establish the Vatican's own chain of communications in the prison camps of South Africa, but found that it might be months before he could get a passage by ship or aircraft to Cape Town. He mentioned this to Derry one day and Derry told Alexander, now field marshal.

"I will get him a plane to go wherever he wishes", said Alexander instantly. O'Flaherty flew to South Africa and set up his organization of priests to compile lists of prisoners and keep the Holy Office informed of sickness or death among them, and then borrowed an aircraft for a second time, to fly to Jerusalem to help with arrangements for the transfer to Israel of many of the Jews whom he had saved from the Germans.

To both O'Flaherty and Derry came Italians with a very different motive—revenge. Many of them dreamt of nothing but exacting retribution from the informers and torturers, particularly the Fascists, and any German SS men that might be caught. Fate had already overtaken Ludwig Koch, who was shot by *partisani* before he could reach Milan. Perfetti and Aldo Zambardi were arrested and thrown into Regina Coeli. When the Romans, impatient that these men had not been executed, threatened, with others, to burn the hated prison and all in it to the ground, these two and other collaborators and informers were moved to jail in Milan and not heard of again. Cipolla, thanks to the Lucidis who, with Derry's agreement, told of the good work he had done at times for the organization, got off with twenty-four years imprisonment. Derry received one of the biggest shocks of his career in Rome one day when a British Foreign Office man showed him a list of renegade British subjects who had worked with the enemy and asked if the organization knew any of them. Derry at once pointed to a name on the list—"I know that one," he said, "but I didn't know he was British. In fact, he worked for us and was one of those left behind when the Germans cleared out of Regina Coeli."

This man, known to the organization as "Jack", had been found by Brother Robert Pace and, as he had his own car and apartment, proved most useful in bringing escapers into Rome, although Derry always felt uneasy about him because, the major reasoned, anyone the Germans permitted to use a car must be helping them in some way. But "Jack" continued to put in first-class work until the day he was arrested. Derry, still suspicious, expected then that he would "do a Perfetti" on them, but the weeks passed and none of the billets he had known were raided. It was eventually discovered that he *had* been tortured by Koch, but divulged not a word.

Derry now told all this to the Foreign Office man, who stared at him in amazement. "But this man", he said, "is the Cockney Broadcaster of Rome!" "Jack" was indeed Italy's equivalent of Germany's "Lord Haw Haw". As the result of Derry's testimony, "Jack" avoided the fate of William Joyce on the gallows, and did not even stand trial. It was decided that he should be interned in Italy until the Allies left the country. He was told that if he ever set foot on British territory anywhere in the world, he would be arrested and tried for treason.

In the three years of its existence the Allied Screening Commission (which grew to a staff of 200) investigated more than 90,000 cases, presented 75,000 certificates of thanks signed by Field Marshal Alexander, and repaid £1,000,000 in cash to those who had loaned money to O'Flaherty and others to help the Allied cause. First to repay the British Government were the Russians, who refunded £25,000. Sir D'Arcy Osborne was determined that the principals should be rewarded in some way also and this was straightforward in most cases—except that of Mrs. Delia Kiernan. The wife of the neutral Irish Minister, she could hardly be expected to accept a British war decoration, especially since her efforts were still secret and were to remain so for years. O'Flaherty, who had a supreme contempt for decorations himself, solved the problem. He suggested to Sir D'Arcy that British Foreign Office funds would no doubt run to a piece of jewelry for the lady and she never need disclose where she got it, or why.

Major Derry, who already had the Military Cross, was awarded the Distinguished Service Order, Lieutenants Simpson and Furman the Military Cross.

O'Flaherty was made a Commander of the British Empire. This medal, together with the U.S. Medal of Freedom with Silver Palm, and his decorations from Haiti and San Domingo, from Canada, Australia and Italy, he sent to his sister, Mrs. Bridie Sheehan, in the small Kerry town of Cahirciveen— and never looked at them again. In 1946 he was promoted from *Scrittore* to be Substitute Notary at the Holy Office. Fathers Galea, Maden and Borg and Brother Robert Pace were made Members of the British Empire, and King George VI "specially commended" Miss Molly Stanley and Fathers Buckley, Claffey, Gatti, Treacy and Lennan. Evangelo Averoff received the Order of the British Empire, Mrs. Chevalier the British Empire Medal.

With peace, O'Flaherty was back out in the streets of Rome once more, traversing the city with his huge strides, bringing news of POWs to Italian families. He was no longer in constant deadly danger but still not entirely free from action.

Some of the newly arrived American troops, who had no idea of the pro-Allied activities of hundreds of priests during the German occupation, took to the habit of jeering in the streets at what they were pleased to call "black beetles". On at least two occasions O'Flaherty, overhearing the remark, promptly knocked the speaker down in the street!

After almost a year confined to the Vatican, O'Flaherty gleefully took down his golf clubs once more and was again a regular player at the course near Ciampino. One day—it was sometime in 1946—he lost a ball and went to look for it. He found himself in a tiny half-ruined village beside the fairway—a few cottages, a damaged church, a bell tower without a bell. A number of ragged, half-starved men, women and children were huddled in what remained of the cottages. They appeared to be Central European refugees, certainly they were not Catholics, and they were too hungry and miserable to be concerned about religion. Ever practical, ever charitable, O'Flaherty told them, "I will be back this afternoon—with food!" He got into his little car and hurried back to Rome where he bought up stocks of food and wine and collected clothing from one of the monasteries. While the refugees were eating, they watched with astonishment. The burly Monsignor stripped off his robe, opened his collar, and started in there and then on the church, carrying out the rubble and rubbish that had accumulated. Fed, the men rose to their feet one by one and began to help him, not really understanding what it was all about. By evening the church was cleared and partly scrubbed. Day after day, in the times he normally would have played golf, O'Flaherty went back to the "village" and wrought a transformation scene in church and refugees.

The church was painted and refurnished by O'Flaherty out of his own pocket; he got a new bell for the tower and then secured the necessary formal ecclesiastical permission to start holding services there and looked after it as if it were his own "parish". He went to American relief organizations and arranged for a regular supply of food and other necessities until the men could find work, and he started instructing them in the Catholic religion—the children, their parents, a few ancient grandparents. He baptized the lot, prepared them for the other sacraments of the Church and at the appropriate time he hired two buses and brought them to St. Peter's itself, where all were confirmed together. Every Sunday and major feast day for the next twelve years O'Flaherty arrived at the village soon after dawn and spent most of the day with his "parishioners", and as the population grew he even had to say two Masses on each Sunday. Apart from one or two priests on whose assistance he had to call as the "parish" expanded, only two men knew of all this work—his chief, Cardinal Ottaviani, from whom he occasionally had to get extra time off, and Pope Pius, who wrote him a special letter of appreciation.

For all those years also O'Flaherty carried out another work of mercy. Colonel Kappler, the Monsignor's archenemy, was among those tried by the Allies for war crimes. He was sentenced to life imprisonment for his part in the Ardeatine Massacre and incarcerated in Gaeta prison between Rome and Naples. Only one person ever visited him in jail— Father O'Flaherty. The Monsignor went to the prison about once a month and even pleaded first with the Allies and later with the Italians to have Kappler freed after six years or so. In March 1959 Kappler was baptized into the Catholic Church by O'Flaherty, who had just been appointed Chief Notary at the Holy Office, but was already ailing and nearing the end of his active career.

For more than twenty years Rome had told tales of O'Flaherty, as boxer, golfer and Pimpernel, some entirely apochryphal, many falling far short of the truth. He was unlucky enough to become a legend in his own lifetime and this in itself, combined with the attitude of some members of the Vatican officialdom, clouded his last years. Not a few of his colleagues and superiors (with the outstanding exception of the redoubtable Cardinal Ottaviani who stood staunchly by him to the end) were bitterly and publicly jealous of his fame—or notoriety, as they would describe it. They looked upon him as an adventurer, a mountebank or, as one American churchman put it, "A jumped-up Irish peasant"! None of these people believed in his motives because they had no experience, nothing that could enable them to comprehend them. Though trained to believe, and to preach that charity is the greatest of all virtues, none of his critics could even begin to understand O'Flaherty's simple—yes, if you like, *peasant*—interpretation of the doctrine "Thou shalt love thy neighbour as thyself." Yet this was what shone through all O'Flaherty's actions—it was the only thing that could explain the varying attitudes and reactions, decisions and exploits of this extraordinary man. With his genuine modesty—perhaps that also was a "peasant" characteristic—O'Flaherty would quite angrily refute flattering suggestions at postwar parties that he had been a hero; he would have been acutely embarrassed to have overheard the comment of a very old nun, the one who used to clean his room at the Collegio Teutonicum. She was roasting coffee beans on the roof of the College when a priest mentioned that O'Flaherty was retiring from Vatican service. "There goes a true saint", she said.

Many others called Hugh O'Flaherty a saint, because they could think of nothing else to explain his character. And nothing is more damaging in ecclesiastical circles than to be canonized while yet alive. O'Flaherty was sadly aware that while he had, quite unconsciously, won the esteem and admiration, indeed the love of thousands of men and women of half the nations of the globe, he was now disliked and distrusted by some at least of his American, Italian and Irish colleagues. "I've suffered too much promotion", he explained to journalists, radio and TV and film producers who sought him out in the immediate postwar years for interviews or help in producing a record of the work of the organization.

When Pope John XXIII ascended the throne of Peter, Rome's raconteurs churned out countless stories, mostly untrue, but few out of character, about *Il Papa*. The one that concerned Pope John and O'Flaherty was a typical example. The story ran that Pope John, who had himself done so much work for escapers and refugees in Greece and Turkey in the early years of the war, saw in O'Flaherty a similar character and decided to reward him for work which, officially at least, the Vatican knew nothing about. Smilingly he told O'Flaherty, "Monsignor, you have had twenty years of *dolce vita* in Rome, it really is high time you did some real work! We will make you a bishop and you can go to work in Africa, for which you were destined when first you came here." So the anecdote went. O'Flaherty could at that time quite easily have pleaded ill health. Instead he was recorded as saying with blunt honesty that he did not think he had the makings of a bishop and, anyway, he wanted to go home to Ireland. The story could very well have been true—it reflected the characters of both men— but it was not correct. In fact, Cardinal Ottaviani and Pope John knew that O'Flaherty was now in the first stages of arteriosclerosis, and in June 1960 he had his first stroke and spent several weeks in the Blue Sisters' hospital in Rome, where he had hidden General Gambier-Parry, before going to Cahirciveen in August and formally retiring from the Holy Office in September. For two years from January 1961, with a holiday interval in Ireland, he worked in Los Angeles in the council, which advises the Archbishop on technical, legal and canonical matters. But his health was deteriorating all the time, and he returned to Cahirciveen at the beginning of 1963. He had a second stroke in May, and died peacefully on October 30 in his front room over the scarlet-painted hardware store owned by his sister in Cahirciveen's West Main Street. He was buried in the Daniel O'Connell Memorial cemetery and with the flowers from his family and Irish friends that lay on the grave were wreaths from Sam Derry, now a retired lieutenant colonel, the Irish Guards headquarters in London, the British War Office, and the British Embassy in Dublin.

One summary of the Pimpernel's character was contained in the obituary notice written for the Mungret College *Journal* by Father Francis Joy, S.J., his fellow Kerryman: "Hugh O'Flaherty was above all a generous honest-to-God Irishman without guile. His big heart was open to any and every distress and he was lavish in his efforts to assuage suffering in any form, a facet of his character which made him an easy target for any hard-luck story. His expenditure on charity must have been immense and his motto always was *Cast your bread upon the waters*. . . . His career in the Vatican service was not without its checks and frustrations. But with his sunny disposition he was proof against such embarrassments. And above all one could say of him that, without ostentation, his life was always ordered to using his powers in fair weather or foul for the glory of God. Can any of us hope to achieve more?"

The Vatican gardens where secret records of the organization were
buried in biscuit boxes.

ILLUSTRATIONS